Fiona Scott-Norman is a freelance writer, columnist, broadcaster, stand-up comic, director and DJ, and back in the day was a comedy and theatre critic for 16 years. At school she was as popular as scabies, a formative experience that inspired her to create this book.

Edited by Fiona Scott-Norman

Affirm Press

Published by Affirm Press in 2011
1 Jacksons Road, Mulgrave VIC 3170
www.affirmpress.com.au

National Library of Australia Cataloguing-in-Publication entry:
Scott-Norman, Fiona.
Don't Peak at High School / edited by Fiona Scott-Norman
978-0-9807904-5-0 (pbk.)
Subjects: Bullying in schools—Australia.
Celebrities—Australia.
371.58

Photographer credits:
Page 18 courtesy of Neil Bennett
Page 118 courtesy of Heath Missen
Page 172 courtesy of Leanne Hanley

Cover designed by Dean Gorissen/Room44
Printed in Australia by Griffin Press

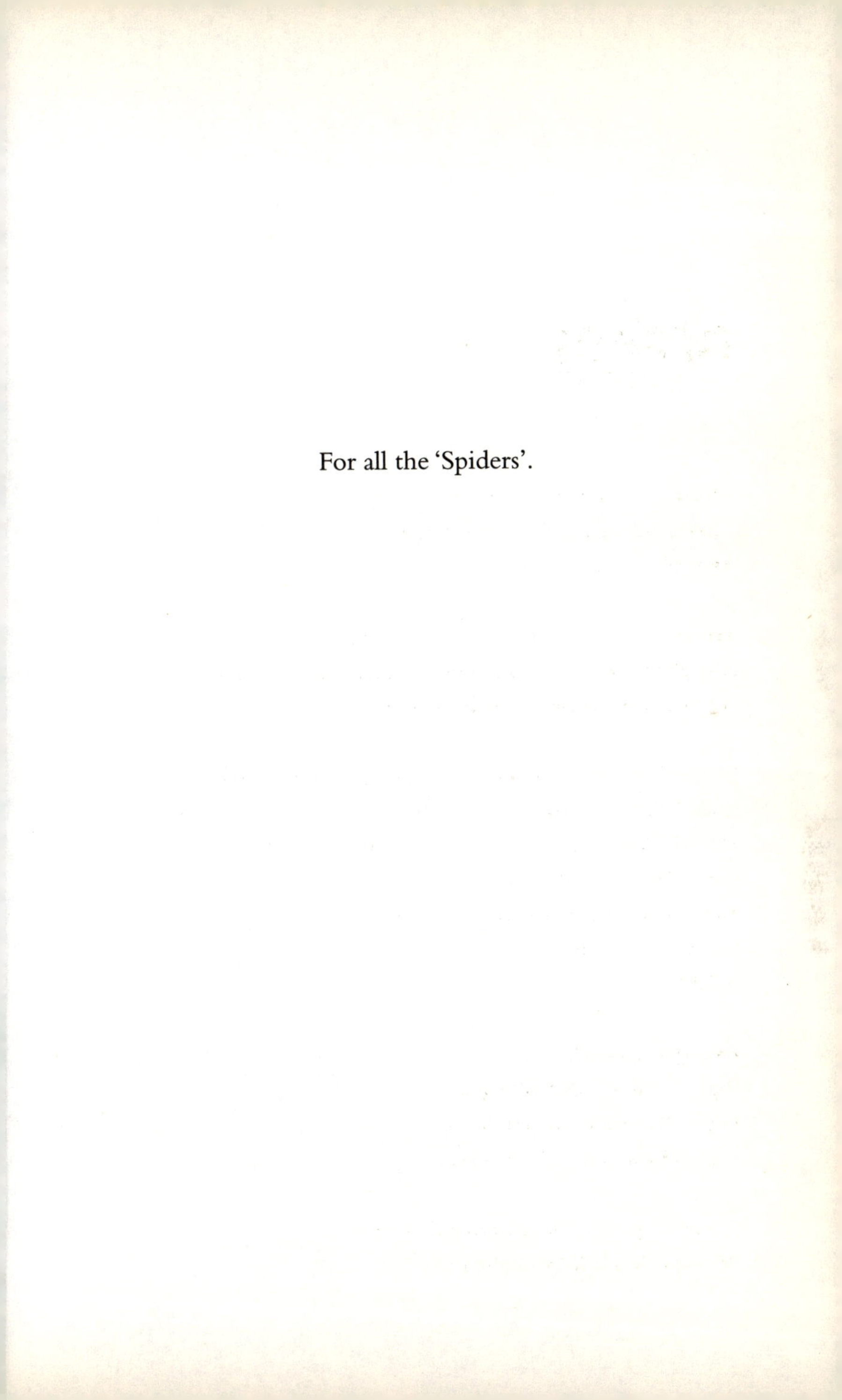

For all the 'Spiders'.

Edited by Fiona Scott-Norman

CONTENTS

INTRODUCTION

There are plenty of well-documented downsides to being bullied at school. The cruelty, the exclusion, and the fact that at some point a well-meaning nong will assure you that, 'Your schooldays are the best days of your life.'

According to recent research from the Australian Federal Government, one in four students is affected by bullying. And if you're part of that oh-so-lucky 25 per cent, if you're spending your days hiding in the toilets to avoid being spat on, or reading the Twitter feed #yournameisuglyandstinks, it's pretty depressing to be informed that this is as good as it's gonna get.

Well, it's not. This book is here to assure you that school is as far from the best days of your life as Wolfgang Amadeus Mozart is from making next year's triple j Hottest 100.

I know this to be true, because my school years sucked, as they did for every person featured herein. *Don't Peak At High School* is a collection of interviews with 15 of the most interesting, talented, accomplished and, yes, *popular* people in Australia. Each of them is successful, an A-lister in their field. But hard though it is to believe now, their school years were 18 parts crapola and they were bullied from pillar to post.

Megan Washington, Tim Ferguson, Charlie Pickering, Kate Miller-Heidke, Bindi Cole, Eddie Perfect, Adam Boland, Paul Capsis, Adam Goodes, Wendy Harmer, Penny Wong, Judith Lucy, Benjamin Law, Marieke Hardy and Brendan Cowell have all generously shone a high-beam torch into the dank, dismal, rat-infested basements of their experiences at school.

To channel Kasey Chambers, no, some weren't pretty enough. Or sporty enough. Or, for that matter, non-poofy enough. They were smacked about and ignored, picked on and picked last, mocked and reviled. And yet, intriguingly, once they left school, they transformed into high-achieving, powerful, charismatic individuals who've forged enviable lives for themselves. This potential is there for everyone.

These are stories not only of survival, but of people who've flourished despite inauspicious beginnings. Coincidence? Not likely.

Some of these stories are more confronting than others, but each is potent, moving and fascinating. There is a cocktail of reasons why someone is vulnerable to being picked out from the pack and set upon, and these interviews recount every which way to have a miserable time. But, more importantly, they offer strategies to cope and conquer, and inspiring and inventive ways to deal with what feels like the undealable. Being bullied shaped these people, and the inference is clear: there are advantages to being unpopular at school, because you are forced to fall back on your own resources.

You may relate most to Megan Washington, who was in her ugly duckling years and wanted to be liked too much, or Judith Lucy, who used humour to cope with fighting parents and toxic school friends. Or perhaps you'll respond to Brendan Cowell, who was way too weird for his school, or Adam Goodes, who escaped racism through sport.

Interestingly, not one of them wishes, with hindsight, that they weren't bullied. This is not to suggest that being bullied is some kind of enviable self-development package, but there's no question that having already been through it, the positives become more apparent.

If there were a magic wand I could wave over my own past, I'd consider rewriting the bit where I was the most unpopular kid at the largest mixed boarding school in Europe, and nicknamed Spider. I was at that place for seven years, there were over 2000 students, and I had people I'd never seen before in my life be mean to me. I was ungainly, I didn't have one boyfriend, everyone hated me, and as an only child I had no idea how to relate to anyone my own age. And they nicknamed me 'Spider' (of all things!).

It was textbook horrendous. I was deeply lonely. And yet, I'm not sure I'd change a thing. It's clear that my most valuable skills, tools and traits, such as my self-reliance and sense of humour, were honed as coping mechanisms to deal with a totally shithouse situation. Because no one was knocking down my door to invite me to midnight feasts and games of Quidditch, I was also free to curl up in a foetal position under the covers and read.

I am now, entirely relatedly, a writer and comedian, and I literally wouldn't be who I am now if it hadn't been for those experiences. This is where the idea for *Don't Peak At High School* came from; I figured I couldn't be the only one who'd discovered Friedrich Nietzsche's theory, 'What does not kill me, makes me stronger.'

The ages of our interviewees range from the early-twenties to nudging 50, which gives a broad representation of age and experience. You get to see how being bullied plays out both in the short-term and over the best part of a lifetime, and the way boys favour biffo, and girls lean towards psychological torture.

It's interesting to note that even though bullying has partly moved online, and tends to be less aggressively physical, the intent and impact remain the same. The reasons for being picked out remain the same. To be bullied is to be bullied is to be bullied.

Although cyber-bullying has added another level of complexity, historically speaking this is one of the best times to be bullied, ostracised or vilified. That kind of behaviour is no longer considered acceptable; there are programs and legislation in place, and help, strategies and support are available. This level of intervention and transparency is *new*.

The best thing you can do for yourself is talk to your parents, talk to your teachers, and keep talking until you get help. This can be tough to do because most unpopular kids feel ashamed: that there's something wrong with *them*, that they deserve it somehow. If you take anything away from this book, perhaps it could be that there's no shame in being bullied – not only are you not alone (one in four, remember!), but also it's happened to the best.

And, if it helps to think of it this way, perhaps only the best of us *are* bullied. Certainly the more unusual someone is, the harder it is to fit in, and the more likely it is the schoolyard will turn on you. But although school, due to a little-known clause in Einstein's Theory of Relativity, appears to last forever, it's an illusion. Before you know it school will be receding in your rear-vision mirror so fast that you'll have to squint to see it.

Then, once you leave school, the individuality that was the albatross around your neck becomes the highly prized and sought-after commodity. There are long-term benefits to being forced to be your own person; no one becomes great by fitting in or disappearing.

Above all else, I hope you find this book, and the stories inside it, valuable and inspiring, and a reminder that if you're #yournameisuglyandstinks at the moment, don't sweat it. There is absolutely nothing to be gained by peaking at high school.

Yours affectionately,
~~Spider~~ Fiona Scott-Norman

EDDIE PERFECT

A couple of things need to be cleared up about Eddie Perfect. Yes, it truly is his real name, and no, despite being handsome, talented and more in demand than the last can of Coke at a beach party, his life has not been an endless procession of Turkish delight, rose petals and perfumed-oil foot massage.

Eddie's a restive spirit, and he refuses to settle in any one discipline. He's widely known as Mick Holland in Channel Ten's comedy series *Offspring*, but he also wrote and starred in the Helpmann Award-winning *Shane Warne: The Musical*, took the lead role of Mack The Knife in Melbourne's Malthouse Theatre production of *The Threepenny Opera*, and in 2011 his satiric solo cabaret show, *Misanthropology*, won plaudits at the Sydney Arts Festival and Melbourne International Comedy Festival.

His refusal to be pigeon-holed as a comic *or* TV actor *or* theatre actor *or* singer-songwriter *or* cabaret performer has a direct lineage back to high school, where every attempt was made to shove this arts-shaped boy into a science-shaped hole. Plain, chubby, artsy and wussy, the young Mr Perfect found school as suffocating as one of those plastic bags you're meant to keep away from toddlers, and has been running in the opposite direction ever since.

“**I remember waiting high school out.** Biding my time. I knew, as soon as it was over, I was going to get the hell out of there and do whatever I wanted. At our last assembly the school captain got up and did his speech, and said, ‘You know they say that high school’s the best years of your life’, and then he broke down and started sobbing. Really crying, really upset, saying, ‘I can’t believe we’re going to leave all this behind. It’s been so amazing.’ I’m looking at him, astounded, thinking, ‘Are you f***ing kidding me? Anything and everything is going to be better than this.’

My school was an all-boys private in Mentone down on the beach. It was a very disciplined place. You lined up, a bell went and you went here. Another bell went and you went there. I wasn’t smoking pot behind the shed going, ‘F*** the rules, man.’ I was very much, ‘I’m going to follow all the rules, and be diligent, and I’m going to play the model student’, but that doesn’t mean I was happy with it. I definitely thought, ‘This is ridiculously shit.’

It was clear that a certain kind of boy was going to be successful, and that that boy was not me. At my school it was all about becoming an engineer. Everyone wanted to be an engineer. I still don’t even know what an engineer is, but lots of people wanted to be one. It was a cricket-in-the-summer, football-in-the-winter kind of place. The arts were not big there. At all. I mean you could *do* it, but it was never taken seriously. There was no music program, and the drama program was so small I didn’t even study it.

Ironically our school motto was '*Per Vias Rectas*', which when you're at an all-boys school sounds bad, but it means, 'By Right Paths'. And the way it was explained to us was there are right paths and there are wrong paths. You can choose your own path … so long as it's engineering.

I was specifically told not to study the things I wanted to, because it wouldn't add up to a decent tertiary entrance score. I was determined to study the humanities whether it was beneficial for my grades or not, and I ended up getting the highest marks in my year, so they were wrong.

I mean, I was doing art in VCE, but I had teachers who, in a free period, would tell me off for working on my folio. In a free period! Telling you to do something serious! My recollection is of plotting and scheming, and *finding* time. I'm still like that. I don't like telling people what I'm up to.

My experience of high school was that it's a very constricted and narrow view of how people are supposed to be. It's particularly limiting and suburban. I was always creative, and wanted to be successful and do something unique, but none of that was ever recognised at school. It was kind of my own shameful little secret. I wanted to have a nose ring early on, and tattoos, and I bought garishly bright retro pants to wear. I'd never wear them now, but I had this need to express myself beyond the very limited means that were available.

I had a very strong inner life, and looking back I was clearly searching for a way to express myself, but I didn't have an avenue. I thought visual art was going to be it, you know, like, 'Here we go, it's something I'm good at it, I can do it on my own, you start with nothing and you create something.' And then I got into art school and discovered that I didn't have anything to say. I still really love visual art, and I can see what's good, but I'll never be good at it myself. It wasn't until I discovered songwriting, five or six years later, that I went, 'Oh, *this* is it.' I love words and music, and I've got ideas and I can express them.

I wasn't cool or popular at all. In the slightest. I was always chubby, even at primary school, and I was a fat kid all the way through high school. I wasn't massively overweight, more chubby, but it just diminishes your attractiveness. I wasn't good-looking either, so I was very much aware of my place. You don't hope for much.

I don't think I fitted in because, essentially, I was a bit of a wussbag. I was sensitive and I'd cry really easily. I wasn't tough, I didn't know how to stick up for myself, and in physical or verbal fights I had no skills. I wasn't confident, I was scared, and I was easily intimidated, which doesn't help. I was arty. I liked music theatre. I did ballet when I was in primary school, and when someone found out about that, as one can imagine, it was pretty excruciating.

I was shithouse at sport. I mean I was okay at basketball but I was really bad at PE. We had a South-East Asian PE teacher, and his nickname for me was 'not so' which he thought was hilarious. Do you see what he did there? 'Not So Perfect.' There was a lot of canoeing on the beach. I remember falling out of the boat in really choppy waters on Port Philip Bay, and him on a megaphone going, 'Get back in the boat, Not So, get back in the boat.' Ah, he hated my guts. I couldn't do a chin-up until I was maybe 25. I just used to dangle from the f***ing monkey bars like a fat idiot.

You just get dismissed, really. It's pretty embarrassing. I can't remember ever being actively picked on about being bad at sport, just being overlooked and ignored. I was just never part of the mainstream. I had this sort of enemy, I don't know why, Patrick someone – I wish I could remember his name, he's a douchebag, that guy – who would for no reason just kind of grab me, twist my arm behind my back at lunch-time and slam my face into the locker. I was an occasional target for him, and I really hated it.

My literature teacher gave me a card at the end of Year 12 with the Robert Frost poem, *The Road Not Taken*. When I read that it was freaking mind-blowing. It was exactly how I felt.

I wasn't at the bottom of the heap. I was *towards* the bottom, but mercifully there were people that were more bullied than me. I had friends, but I didn't ever like them particularly; they were allies I guess, but we had no shared interests. I found them increasingly embarrassing and stifling – there was an alpha male in the group I didn't get on with – and I thought the whole hierarchy thing was ridiculous.

As I got towards Years 11 and 12 I extricated myself from them, to pretty much no one. It wasn't an unhappy withdrawal, I didn't feel lonely. I spent most of my lunchtimes in the art room working on my folio rather than having to deal with hanging out in the schoolyard and that dynamic.

I got on really well with adults, and I had good art, history and literature teachers, so I threw myself into the work. The bonus was I learned to love the learning, and the teachers that liked me encouraged me. My literature teacher gave me a card at the end of Year 12 with the Robert Frost poem, *The Road Not Taken*. When I read that it was freaking mind-blowing. It was exactly how I felt.

If I think about it, most of my formative events were being rejected by girls that I liked, and being really hurt by that. It happened every time. I had the hots for this girl, Zoe, and I got up the courage to ask her to my Year 12 formal. And when we got there, within five minutes, she was getting it on with my archenemy Patrick. That sort of thing happened a lot.

I had sisters, so I was really good at talking to girls, and not good at exploiting them, which is 99 per cent of how you get by with girls at high school. I didn't feel right about taking advantage, so I'd always, eventually, become their friends. Or we'd be friends first and it would never become anything else because they value your friendship. You know. One of those guys.

Our school finally had a musical, and I got into that in Year 11. It was amazing because I got to meet girls doing something I was actually good at. That changed everything.

I was making a kind of headway during that process. Until one day. I used to ride my bike home past the bus stop where all the girls from the local schools converged. There would be at least 200 girls there every afternoon, and it was the most hideously self-conscious stretch of road I'd ride along. To them I was just some twat in a blazer, they wouldn't have looked twice, but I always felt like 200 pairs of eyes were on me.

Then one time, after the musical, I was riding home with my helmet on the handlebars – because it wasn't cool to wear a helmet – and I thought I'd ride without my hands on the handlebars. So I'm cycling no-hands-no-helmet past this bus stop, and then, like a miracle, this girl yells out, 'Hey, Eddie!' I'm like, 'Is this possible?' And it's a pretty, popular girl from the musical waving at me, so I kind of turned around, waved, and rode into the back of a parked car.

I didn't even break my fall with my hands. I smashed my face into the back windscreen, the bike crumpled in half, I hit the deck, and 200 girls just pissed themselves laughing. And you know when you're hurt but you pretend that you're not, and you leap up really quickly and pretend that it's all okay? Well, I leapt up straight away, but I was in agony, because those gears that are kind of like bunny ears, one of them had stabbed me right in the scrotum, I'd hurt my leg so much that I couldn't put my weight on it, and I'd actually cracked the windscreen with my face. And I couldn't ride away because the frame was buckled, so I had to pick up my bike and limp away from 200 laughing girls.

Yeah. So that undid all the good work I'd done. It was like, 'I've got to move towns. Now.'

What motivated me a lot, and probably still motivates me, was the getting out. I hated Mentone. Really hated it. I hated food courts, and tenpin bowling alleys, and that whole community vibe. My dad was a school teacher, and well-liked, so we were very much a part of the 'community' – people knowing what's going on, and keeping tabs on you, and all that kind of stuff. I wanted to find my *own* community. I was working at an education bookstore during the holidays, stacking shelves, and thinking, 'I've got to get away from this.'

Shane Warne: The Musical was the first thing I did, finally, accidentally, that Mentone would be vaguely interested in. I got asked to sing the National Anthem for the Boxing Day tests, and the effect that had on people from Mentone was full-on. Like all of a sudden I'd somehow combined all of my artistic wankery with sport, and it blew people's minds – people were ringing up my family in tears. It was the pinnacle of success to them.

It was kind of a funny moment, but it also made me realise I don't give a shit. From school I was originally motivated by, 'I'll be a success, and I'll stick it up all of you and show you', but now I don't care. I don't do it for that reason at all any more. But everyone's motivated by something, and if you're lucky – and I consider myself lucky – you find a medium that you really love and are genuinely interested in.

The other motivation was girls. I wasn't good-looking enough, or sporty enough, to fit in, and I realised that if I wanted to get anywhere with girls I'd need to develop some skills. I was also going to use my skills to get out, and not in a noisy way. I was never arrogant. I just knew I was going to do my own thing and one day it would work out.

One flow-on from school, because the dreams I had weren't considered aspirational, is that I've got an almost pathological fear of talking about my projects with other people. Letting people know somehow seems to diminish it. You know how people are curious about what other people think about them? I'm terrified. I will do everything to avoid finding out what people think about me, because I've built up such a strong thing about not giving a shit. That protects me, but it also doesn't invite in any possible nice things. I don't even really know what my friends think about me, and as soon as people start talking about me I get really uncomfortable.

I remember making an actual decision to not be shy, to work on being better with people. I used to read books on it, like Dale Carnegie's *How to Win Friends and Influence People*. It was good, because the principle of it is 'Show a detailed interest in other people' and it works. The only problem is you then get into conversations with people about things you don't give a shit about, and it'll bore you to death.

I think the institution of high school is, at its core, about early detection. It worries me. I think high school is getting so career-focused. They want to form you and then send you off in a particular direction. I resisted that entirely, and I resisted it by just shutting the hell up. But what I've learned from that is I listen to my gut. I go, 'This feels right', or 'This doesn't feel right.' I don't make a song and dance about it, but I extricate myself when it's not me. I don't pledge allegiance to anyone, because I feel constrained when I'm with just one group of people. I really love doing comedy, and it's given me the most opportunities out of any industry I've worked in, but I don't say 'I'm a comedian' and just live in that world.

I like to be able to do stuff, and I don't like people telling me I can't. I'm very sensitive to criticism or even the slightest comment – I fear even just listening. How does any one person know what another person's potential could be? Even in general conversation, people can shape your mind and the way you think about yourself and your possibilities.

It happens a lot, even the people you love the most can damage you with a very narrow view of what you're capable of doing. People are really worried about what people think of them, and that probably holds them back more than anything else. My way of getting around that has been avoiding people's opinions. Or just telling them, 'F*** you, I'm going to do it anyway.'

I've got no qualifications to write music, I've got no qualifications to write scripts, or even do comedy. I found all of it terrifying, but I made myself do it, because I thought

I *might* be able to do it. And I meet *heaps* of people who go, 'Oh I'm not a writer', or 'I'm not a songwriter', and I don't know why they made that decision. I don't have any right to call myself anything, except I've done it a lot, and now it's just accepted.

I feel sick going back to my high school. It's a weird place. It's not traumatic and it's not painful, it's just so uninteresting. It's just ... bleugh. You know The Nothing in *The Neverending Story*? It was like this beige, indescribable cardigan coming for you, and if you're not able to run away and escape it, it's going to envelop you, and you're going to become beige like everybody else.

So you've just gotta run. And put your fingers in your ears, and go 'Lalalalala', and do what you want, and not worry about what other people think. It might make me seem detached or aloof or difficult to know, but it's certainly helped me do what I wanted to do. I think the title of this book is absolutely right. School is such a tiny part of life. It can be really great for some people, or it can be really horrific, but even the worst things, like riding into a parked car, can actually become funny.

And you're not going to remain that person. When I was in Year 12, I saw a piece of pottery in the window of the school library, this really shit ceramic pot, saying 'Eddie Perfect Year 7', and I never could remember making that pot. Obviously I must have, but we're all a bit like that f***ed up pot – once you leave, you're not the person you were in high school any more.

School's the best catch-all system they can churn people through. Some people will get bumped or squashed, and not everyone's going to come out perfectly. But once you get out you can do whatever you like. That's why I find it hard to talk about school. I kind of don't want to acknowledge the past at all, because I prefer to diminish it and take its power away. I draw a line, like, 'Done. Whatever. Move forward.' ”

I shall be telling this with a sigh
Somewhere ages and ages hence:
Two roads diverged in a wood, and I,
I took the one less traveled by,
And that has made all the difference.

From *The Road Not Taken* by Robert Frost

MEGAN WASHINGTON

There are a few words you could use to describe singer/songwriter Megan Washington; uncompromising, idiosyncratic and a little bit sweary. That's a large part of her charm – she's literate as all get-out, but splendidly uninhibited when it comes to mixing the four-letter words with the four-syllable ones.

Mostly though, 24-year-old Megan is profoundly creative, dynamic, a bit gorgeous and as focused as a Bond villain's deathray. And her career is kicking along very nicely, thank you. She was the undisputed highlight of the 2010 ARIA Music Awards, singing 'Sunday Best' and bringing some desperately needed pizzazz, star quality and glamour to an event that redefined lacklustre.

She also took out the gong for Breakthrough Artist, and nudged out Our Kylie for Best Female Artist. Her first album, *I Believe You Liar*, went platinum in January 2011, two days before she and her band, the eponymous Washington, scored three songs in triple j's Hottest 100. She's doing okay for the chubby, awkward girl who was transplanted from Papua New Guinea to Brisbane at 11, who nobody would sit next to, and who bribed kids with Chupa Chups to be her friends.

Her self-proclaimed downfall was that she wanted to be liked too much, so put up with anything in the hope of being included. After years of unsuccessfully trying to please everybody else, including a short but highly successful career as a jazz singer covering classics and standards, she's now deliriously herself, winning acclaim for her kooky, intelligent pop music.

“**What was so hard** was finding myself washed up in a place where reason and rationality had no existence. My tools didn’t work. My intelligence didn’t work. Because no one gave a flying rat’s arse unless you were wearing Billabong or Quicksilver and had shiny blonde hair. The only thing that worked was being the girl everybody wants to know, which I wasn’t.

As far as I’m concerned, my life began at 18. Okay, it started when I was born, but that part finished at 11, when we moved from PNG, and then from 11 to 18 it was a whole effort to get the f*** out of there. In PNG everything was pretty good. I was happy. Then I went to a state school for a year in Brisbane. It was just awful. I didn’t understand half the swear words, I didn’t understand what they were calling me. I remember this girl said that my mother was a fat pig. I found that really disturbing, that even your parents weren’t off-limits.

When I was younger I was always very changey, a chameleonic kind of person, but I couldn’t make it work at this school. All the kids were rough. *Rough.* And I’d never experienced physical danger before. One girl on the same softball team was really bad. I mean, I was sporty, I wasn’t a nerd. But she used to just throw the softball *at* me, aim it *into* me.

When I arrived at school in the morning people would throw their bags at me, and food at me, and call me bad names, and then we’d go into class. No one would sit with me because apparently I stank. And I wasn’t to answer any questions, because that was to draw attention to myself, you know, so I never put my hand up because then everyone would look at me and remember that they hated me. So I'd get through class somehow, usually by ignoring everything, and then there'd be morning tea. I'd take my morning tea and find places to just walk, usually to the primary school area where the others weren't.

It was the psychology of it that was weird. Girls would say things like, 'My friend wants to ask you out on a date', and then everyone would laugh. And that's really a mindf***, as an 11 or 12 year old, because 'My friend wants to date you', that's a positive statement, right? But when it's followed by laughter... I remember feeling very confused most of the time. Not ever understanding what was going on. Entire mountains and valleys of all this subtext.

It made no sense, because a year before, in PNG, I'd been totally normal. Normal! At that school everybody liked me, I had friends, we hung out and did stuff, and now I stank, and had a fat pig mother, and ... I couldn't understand. I kept wondering what it was about me that made me so repulsive or threatening.

I used to go to the library, and hang out with kids younger than me sometimes, and, because we lived close by, I ran away from school constantly. And I had to see a f***ing counsellor, and it became *my* fault, because to deal with it my reaction was to become very angry and quite aggressive.

A year later I went to an all-girls private school, and the same thing happened. I thought once I went to a different school it would be okay, but when I got to Year 8 it was all f***ed again. The difference was the bullying was now no body, all brain.

I was short and chubby and awkward and had braces, but I was in the popular girl group. I can see now I was only there as the comic relief, they kept me in the group for sport. They all had names like Cheryl and Candace and Vanessa, and at the time I thought they were my friends. But at lunchtime they'd sit with me in a circle and say something like, 'We really need to talk to you about your appearance.' And they'd talk about how when I didn't shave my legs it was disgusting. And how I was getting pimples, and also a little bit fat, and not in a kind way. I mean, that's not kind.

Once, when we were in Grade 10, they said, 'There's a party on Friday, everybody's going, you should come', all welcoming and warm, and emailed or texted me the address. So, on Friday, they were like, 'We'll see you tonight, yeah, bye, yeah', and I came home from school, and had a shower, and got all dressed up, and I got my dad to drive me. I think he left work early so he could drive me. And … the address was just a fish and chip shop, a gap between houses, something. Then it was just me and Dad driving back, in silence.

The dumb thing was I wanted to stay in that group. I don't know why, but I did. I guess I thought it was better to be the worst house in the best street. I'd rather be in this cool group no matter what.

My undoing was that I had this desperate, fundamental urge to be liked. If I'd been happy to mind my own business, to adopt the loser crown and just wear it, I would have avoided a lot of the shit. After a while I did settle into this area of … well, I used to stop at the servo and buy lollies and share them all the time, just to have a friend.

I thought it was better to be the worst house in the best street. I'd rather be in this cool group no matter what.

I was totally unwilling to accept that people didn't like me. They thought I was 'X, Y, Z', and I was like, 'I'm not! I'm not! I'm not! I'll show you! I'll show you! I'll show you!' I couldn't just say, 'I'll only know you for the next five years, and then I'll never see you again', because when you're at school, five years is an *eternity*.

I used to *dread* Mondays. I remember thinking that I would prefer to die, actually physically die, than go back to school next year. I would rather have a life-threatening illness and be in hospital for a year, than go back there. I just hated it all. Every minute of it. I lived in the sick bay. It's a wonder I passed half my classes. The nurses were the most compassionate people in the whole school. They knew. They'd say, 'Have a Panadol and a lie down, darling', and they might even slip you a *Women's Weekly* under the pillows.

The only lucky thing was that I had an extracurricular life, my dancing. There was no one at ballet school from my real school, so I could be myself there. And I was good, and in ballet class that's the only thing that matters. I spent more and more hours there, and I'd leave school early to have private lessons.

I asked my parents a thousand times to take me out of that school. I'd rather be nowhere than somewhere shit – you know how shit coffee is worse than no coffee? I tried so many things. My first plan was that if I did well academically, people would like me, and it became all about hiding in the library the whole time. That didn't work, and besides, I'm an extrovert and I got bored.

The next way I tried to come back from being so ostracised, from being so deeply unhappy, lonely and sad, was by being outrageous – so naughty, so bad, that you got respect that way. I was Charlie Chaplin with a bad attitude. The most slovenly dressed, tough, note-passing, joke-telling, face-pulling, slapstick, loud, you name it. It kind of worked because people knew who I was, but they still didn't like me.

So I became a terror. A really naughty kid. I was suspended a hundred times. I'd not turn up to my exam because it was more dramatic not to go. I got lots of detentions. One teacher used to pick fights with me in class. Every day. For like two terms. Then one day we got into an argument, it escalated, it got more and more heated, she threw a whiteboard eraser at my head, so I just picked up a chair and put a crack in the whiteboard.

That was the start of the fourth term in Year 10, and the school said, 'Don't come back for the rest of the term.' I had eight weeks off, and they just sent me the exams at home. Mum had a lot of trouble getting me into another school, because they were like, 'We don't want her.' Mum had to *beg* this woman at another school who eventually said, 'We'll give her a term and we'll see what happens.'

And then I went to a new school and it was fine. It was full of nerds, every other reject from every other school. It had a performing arts bent, I had a complete shift, and my dancing became my focus.

But I'm grateful for my background now. I'm glad that I experienced the worst, worst, worst when I was 13, 14, 15, because nothing I encounter will ever be as bad. Being bullied has given me tools. Hard-won, amazing tools.

I learned that compromising doesn't work. I'm comfortable making the hard choices, and not being part of any institution. The advantage, when you've never been invited to be part of anything, is I don't give a toss who likes me or who doesn't. People who blog about me and say, 'She's this and she's that and why is she wearing safety glasses?', it doesn't bother me at all. You put no stock in the things that the general population care about. I could not give a flying rat's arse about tit implants or any of that stuff. I'm comfortable with looking like a nine-year-old boy, because that's how I look.

It's really affected how I do business. I only hire, or work with, people I genuinely like or respect, and who like and respect me. I'd never go with a label or manager who had something over me, or bullied me, or tried to influence me in any way. I don't need to make friends that I don't want. I emit a different frequency to most people. A frequency that is 'whatever'. It's made me quite unsentimental. Pragmatic. You know, 'I'm going to have to fire you. Sorry about that.'

And I've learned about power itself, because I know how much power I gave to those people. I gave them everything.

I think being bullied gives you power, because it steels you. It forges you at a really early age, and it makes you strong and hard and ready. I don't know if I could do what I do now, in the fashion I'm doing it – which is with no time, no money, no nothing – if I didn't have a steeliness.

And I've learned about power itself, because I know how much power I gave to those people. I gave them everything. So I know how much power there is to be had. It's a currency, and I understand how humans deal in it.

And it forces you to *really* know yourself. It forces you. I remember I used to talk to myself, because, like, you need to talk through what's happening, and you don't have any friends. So I really got to know myself, because I talked to myself all the time.

I would undramatise everything that happened: take the emotion out and go, 'It was just a physical punch in my physical face, it doesn't mean anything.' Or, 'It was just a name, and that name is just two words, and the words have four letters each, which come from the Greek root, blah blah.' I'd totally abstract the event, which made it dealable. That way of thinking about things has really influenced me, the ability to compartmentalise every terrifying situation into something that can't hurt me.

The best thing was when I suddenly realised I wasn't ugly – it was the most liberating thing in the whole world. I'd believed it for a very, very long time, and then it was, 'I'm not ugly! I don't smell! In fact, I smell great!' I can really appreciate my youth now. I'm 24, and I look pretty good. It's a great feeling, to be able to own myself. Everything that I am, is just where I want to be, and I don't do a single thing that I don't want to do.

I do think being bullied makes you special. You don't get to join in, so it makes you a very idiosyncratic human being, very distinctive. You're special because you really have no other option, and it's also why you get singled out. I learned to embrace my uniqueness, and cultivate, develop and explore it.

The irony, the *irony*, is that the majority of people who are admired and respected in the world, probably came from this kind of background. All the cool kids go out and get drunk, and go to gigs, and parties, and music festivals, and have a great time. And the nerds, the people who were ostracised and unpopular, are at home listening to records, reading books, playing guitar, engorging themselves on culture, and then, bam, they're Tame Impala, they're massive, and all the cool kids are going to go see them. I never went to anything cool, I was always at home reading books and writing songs about my feelings. The first time I went to a Big Day Out, I was 23 and playing at it!

If you look around at the individuals that people like and follow, it's always the people who are so not normal. People like Lady Gaga and Paul Capsis and Oprah. They're not Joe and Mary Average, they're unusual, a rare species of human, and that's why people gravitate. The most individual people are the most interesting, and they're the ones who never fitted in. A lot of people have really dull lives, and I know, because all the bitches found me on Facebook last year and tried to friend me, and they're all working at their dad's plumbing firm, or married and living in the 'burbs.

Look, if you spend most of your school years going out and doing what everybody else does, you'll always do what everybody else does. I'm so glad I didn't peak at high school. I don't want to peak. Not until I'm 65.

I'll be writing musicals for Broadway or other cool shit. I'm going to make *my* music, make *my* art, write *my* pieces, be *me*. It can be difficult to be distinctive, to own that, but when it's difficult then I think, well, it's all I've got. Me. ”

WENDY HARMER

There's only one thing steelier than Wendy Harmer's world-class wit, and that's her strength of will. She's more driven than *Top Gear,* more focused than a bomb-disposal expert, and so determined to succeed that Robert the Bruce's spider looks like a quitter by comparison.

It's 20 years since Wendy, one of Australia's most famous comedians, hosted the ABC's flagship live comedy show *The Big Gig*, after an earlier career as a political journalist. She went on to anchor the breakfast show on Sydney's top-rating radio station 2Day FM for 11 years, in an industry so competitive it makes *MasterChef* look like an afternoon buttering toast.

Wendy's also written six books for adults, including *It's a Joke, Joyce*, *Nagging for Beginners*, *Farewell My Ovaries* and *Friends Like These*; a novel for teens, *I Lost My Mobile at the Mall*; and 15 books for children in the *Pearlie the Park* series. Oh, she's also a lead columnist for *The Sunday Telegraph*, has written two plays, and the libretto for Baz Luhrmann's production of Opera Australia's *Lake Lost*. Wendy pays as much mind to her limitations as most of us do to ants in someone else's kitchen.

It's the same system she used to deal with bullies at school. Born with a severe bi-lateral palate and lip, Wendy attracted more pointing and jostling than a visiting Royal. Faced with the options of 'deal with it' or 'deal with it', she dealt – and the strategies she learned to propel and protect herself have landed her in career clover ever since.

“**I remember coming home** from school at about eight years old and telling my mother the kids were picking on me. She said to go and stand in front of the mirror and, ‘When you can find something to complain about, you come back and tell me.’

There was a fair bit to complain about, actually, because my face was stitched up in a fairly rudimentary fashion when I was born, and I didn’t have the rest of the surgery till I was 14. But I went to the mirror that day, and searched my face, and in the end I wasn’t game to come out and say, ‘Well, there’s this, this and this.’ So I just got on with it, I suppose.

When I looked in the mirror I saw very beautiful, shiny black hair. And I saw lovely big eyes. And then I saw a very flat nose with two wonky nostrils, and a sort of half a lip and, well, my teeth were mangulated and crooked – it wasn’t a good look.

There were insults thrown around. The kids called me, ‘flat-face’, and ‘eagle-beak’, and ‘Wendy the Witch’. As everybody knows, there are the pretty girls in school, and you quickly realise you’re not one of them. On a daily basis I’d have to deal with people staring at me on the bus, and little kids going, ‘Mum, what happened to that girl?’ Looks, and stares, and pointing, and kids, and everyone I met asking, ‘What happened to you?’

People who meant well would say, ‘If it wasn’t for that, you would have been really beautiful.’ My sister really *is* beautiful; she worked as a model for a while [Helen was Penthouse Pet of the Year in 1981]. I'd be standing in front of a mirror as a teenager, getting ready to go out and thinking I looked sort of okay, then she'd come and stand behind me looking so utterly beautiful and I'd be thinking, 'Oh god, there's really no point!' Really, I had to laugh about it in the end.

But, it was hard. My mother left home when I was ten, so Dad brought us up for quite a few years, and we moved school a lot. I was always the kid in the wrong colour uniform, with the cleft palate, with no mother, whose father was a teacher. Gosh, there was a lot of walking into classrooms in the wrong uniform and being the funny-looking kid.

I dealt with it by not registering how people reacted to me. I didn't take any notice. What would be the point? I refused to acknowledge it. I took my seat and looked at the teacher and got on with my work. I knew the bullying was there, I knew the potential for it lurked everywhere, but I couldn't let it in. So, yes, maybe I was bullied and pushed around and stuff, but I blocked it out. I couldn't brook it, so I developed other strategies to get round it.

The fact that you're so different doesn't dawn on you for a while. It probably started in the later years of primary school. In the first couple of schools I was at, Dad was the headmaster, and then in later years he was one of the senior teachers. So I couldn't be picked out as *really* low on the pecking order.

Not that he would protect me, at all! He was very firm with me. He'd just say, 'Get out there and get on with it.'

If I said kids were picking on me he'd say, 'Oh, well, you'll deal with it, you know how to deal with that.' I was never allowed to feel sorry for myself. It just wasn't an option. With the cleft palate nothing was going to change in the short-term, and I was told from when I was very young that I couldn't stay home and cry all day. Dad was very determined that I wasn't going to be a sook and run to him every time something went wrong.

With the cleft palate nothing was going to change in the short-term, and I was told from when I was very young that I couldn't stay home and cry all day.

I coped by being incredibly rational about it. I became very, very rigorous in my mental self-discipline. I'd say, 'I'm not going to let this situation get out of control.' I spent a lot of time thinking, talking to myself, saying, 'You can't let this get you down, you must have courage, you must keep your head up, you must keep going.' That took a lot of time and energy when I was a child. I just had to dust myself off, stand up every day and do it all again until normalcy became a reality for me.

My father would also push me to be out the front, like the time he chose me to be the soloist in the 600-strong combined schools choir in a cathedral. When we had visitors at home, he would get me to stand on the table and read from the newspaper or sing to everyone – I've always had quite a good singing voice.

He just engendered this self-belief in me. I mean, he wanted me to be Australia's first woman prime minister. I now, absolutely, 100 per cent expect that any situation I am put in I am going to do well and I seem to have had a steely core of confidence from when I was born. My mother had a nervous breakdown and attempted suicide on a couple of occasions. I came to see that I was stronger than her. I mothered my own mother, in a way.

I've got no idea how my father managed to stay the course with me in the way he did. Years later, I asked him why he was so tough on me, and he cried. He said, 'It hurt me so much, but I couldn't see any other way. We knew you were going to have a pretty difficult time of it, so we had to toughen you up.' I think he was pretty extraordinary, actually, because I couldn't do it. If it were one of my children being picked on, I'd keep them out of school, and want to run down there and punch all the mothers and kick all the kids.

The most difficult time for me was at 14 when I had the major surgery. They took a skin graft from my lower lip, then stitched it into my upper lip and to keep the skin graft alive, they had to partially sew my mouth together for three months. I had more than 100 blue stitches in my face and I remember my aunt fainting when she saw me at the hospital. I remember very clearly the day I had to go back to school. I was standing by the side of the road waiting for the bus to come, really dreading it, and I had to get on and walk up the aisle of the bus with my new face, with these really red, angry scars.

I'd always dreamed that this operation was going to turn me from Wendy the Witch into Wendy the Beautiful Princess, but it didn't. I just looked slightly better, which was devastating. I had really believed there would be this magical transformation. So … there was nothing to do but push on. That just took an incredible amount of effort. It took every available piece of my will as a human being, every fibre of my body to walk up those steps and onto the bus.

But what other option was there? I'd been brought up in a household where I wasn't allowed to be a victim. There was nowhere to hide, and no one to listen to me whinge. I couldn't use it as an excuse for not doing things.

In the end I think that people accepted me. They'd just say, 'Oh there's Wendy Brown, that'd be right, she'd be the one mucking around or putting her hand up or talking loudly.' I had to crash through and that meant taking part in class and making friends. I'd yack away to the person next to me, and act the goat, and it would be fine. I became an extrovert. No one *could* give me the victim role because I didn't recognise it for myself.

I went to daggy old public schools, and I hung with the misfits in the middle. They were fairly unsophisticated girls from the country, the dumpy girl with the frizzy hair, and then there were the twins, and one of them had a lazy eye… They looked daggy, but they were good girls and we did well in our studies. I found them a really nice group to hang with. And … I loved school, because I just loved learning. I was good at it, and clever and smart, so off I'd go.

I've got two younger brothers and my sister, and they used to regularly bash people up for me! They were incredibly fierce on my behalf. The four of us worked as a really, really tight little group, because we were always under the threat of perhaps having to go to an orphanage and be split up, because after Mum left, Dad told us it might not be possible to keep us all.

I thought I had the ability to bend the world to the way I wanted it to go. I really, really did believe that if I concentrated hard enough, I could make any situation go the way I wanted. I used to sit there and concentrate on making people do the things I wanted them to do. I thought I had some kind of weird power.

I look back at that, and realise it was about control. In the way that anorexics control their bodies and starve themselves, well, for me I wanted control of social situations and how people dealt with me, and so that's where I put a lot of my effort.

Another strategy I developed at school, which I found out later is a well-known yogic technique, is if I'm feeling depressed or whatever, instead of letting it keep going, I sit and think, 'Why do I feel like this?' And I trace it back to the source of what happened, and work through it until I can understand it, get past it and move on. I taught myself to say, 'Why do I feel like this? What's happened? Does that person actually have the capacity to hurt me? Does it make me any less loved?'

I had to be very vigorous with 'counting my blessings', looking beyond my face and saying 'Well, I've got a big heart and a good brain.' It's still something I practice every day. I contemplate what's good about my life, and how fortunate I am. This is not by happenstance – it's important to have some real mental discipline about the way you live your life. You're training yourself every day to be a strong person. If you don't have a good, strong dialogue with yourself, then you can spin out of control. It's almost like you hold your own hand.

I became very good at reading people; it gave me a pretty high EQ (Emotional Quotient), and that's probably what makes me a good comic, journalist and writer. I'm (mostly) able to understand people's motives, and I'm a trained observer. It comes from all that concentration as a child, always sitting just slightly outside and analysing what's going on, because that made it safer for me.

I'd sum things up – 'Who's an enemy? Who's a problem? Who could be a good friend for me?' I've gone through life like that, summing up things, and looking around. Perhaps I'm slow to really commit to people and I know that I can be annoyingly independent.

Perhaps it came from my father's encouragement, but I've always pushed myself to do the hardest things. I wanted to be in the school play, I wanted to have the most handsome boyfriend, and I wanted to be the one that stood up in class and asked questions. It went right through my career, even to stand-up comedy, where I was pushing myself to do the hardest thing. And every time I felt like I was too shy, I'd just make myself do it. You know, to get past all those demons.

Early on, a comedy producer said to me, 'I think you've just got to get used to the idea that you'll never be on television.' However I was cast in *The Gillies Report* and then won the hosting job on *The Big Gig*. Fortunately I've had champions all the way too, but I still have the insecurity of having to prove myself. I way, way overcompensate when I don't have to.

One of my motivations for doing stand-up was definitely, 'I want you to look past my face, and hear what I've got to say.' And also, 'If you're going to stare at me, you might as well have a good look!' Once I became a recognisable face, I had the great thing of never knowing whether people were staring at me because I had scars on my face, or because I was famous. So it worked. It was a good compensation.

When I was hosting *The Big Gig* they used to get all these horrible letters about me, and the show's producer, Ted Robinson, used to steal and hide them. One day I found the whole lot. The most awful one said, 'Did you cut yourself shaving?'; it was like 'Whoa.' Really devastating. But then there's a show next week – what are you going to do?

I'm still bending the world to how I want it to go, and that's why writing is fantastic. I'm a columnist with *The Sunday Telegraph*, which I love, because I'm in control of the way the words go down. If you look at all my work, there's a theme there. I write books, I'm on the radio, I do stand-up and in all these mediums there's little interference. When I was doing *The Big Gig*, I was in control of my contribution. All my work and all my life has been about controlling the situation that I'm in.

I did an audition for [film director] Jane Campion, and I absolutely hated it because I had to do what she told me. I only performed in one play, and I *hated* that because I wasn't in control – all I wanted to do was walk out and say, 'Gidday, it's me! Hi! Anyone here from Footscray?' I've had the chance to write movie scripts, and I probably won't write them, because I know they'll be taken away from me. That's not to say that I don't like collaborating with other people, but my dogged work ethic is often hard for others to deal with.

My son Marley is exactly like me: he has to be the boss, and it's really funny to watch. When he was little, his favourite outfit was a throne and crown and robes, and he would have two of his little girl cousins massaging his feet and bringing him food.

I've always felt there are two kinds of comedians: those who've had abnormal upbringings, and who are desperate to be normal, and those who've had safe, middle-class childhoods who are desperate to turn into rebels. Comedy normalised me; I do routines about ordinary things. I've never got up on stage and talked about my trials and tribulations. I didn't want to set myself up as some kind of freak show. I'll talk about it on a serious level, but I'll never do comedy about it, because there's not a lot there that I find amusing, to tell you the truth.

Funnily enough, when I was on *Australian Story* and did talk about all this, I had many letters telling me, 'We never even noticed you had something different about you.' So there you go, maybe all my strategies worked, or maybe I gave myself a hard time for no good reason.

I often wonder, if I hadn't had the cleft palate, if I'd be a comic. If I'd looked anything like my sister, and with my love of current affairs, I probably would have pursued a media career, done a Jana Wendt. But would I have been a performer? I really don't think I would have. I think the move into performing was definitely to get the monkey off my back. I expect I would have been less driven. It's quite interesting, isn't it? When you ask anybody with a real disability – because mine's not – 'Would they rather not have it?', they're often very ambivalent. In the end, it's our differences that make us who we are. ”

MARIEKE HARDY

Marieke Hardy was never going to have a quiet life. The granddaughter of Frank Hardy and grandniece of Mary Hardy, she is the third generation of one of Australia's most influential cultural and creative dynasties. That she's turned out to be an actor, scriptwriter, columnist, blogger, broadcaster, pot-stirrer and cast-iron minx is no more a surprise than the news that Matt Preston quite likes his tucker.

Confident, eloquent, fiesty and brazen, Marieke doesn't seem a likely candidate for bullying, but it transpires that being precocious and appearing on national television doesn't necessarily pave the road to popularity town. As an only child growing up tutored on film sets, and charming the pants off grown-ups, Marieke was ill-equipped to cope with the psychological machinations of private-schoolgirl infighting.

She's now a successful television scriptwriter, creating *Last Man Standing* and 2011's mordant *Laid*; an award-winning blogger; former co-host of triple j's breakfast show; has several books on the go; and is a panellist on ABC1's *First Tuesday Book Club*. But it's as a political, sexual and cultural provocateur that she has to regularly withstand witheringly toxic, electronic abuse. Marieke credits Years 7 and 8 – what she describes as the 'kill or be killed' years – as giving her the thick skin and fearlessness required to hack out a career as an unflinching public commentator.

“**I grew up in a very confident,** happy world. I got taken out of school a lot, because I travelled overseas with my parents, and went on tour with them when they were filming. I was tutored on set. Then, in Grade 5, I started acting and doing *Henderson Kids Two*, so I was out of school for six months. But they diligently kept me up with my schoolwork, and I never had issues coming back and fitting in.

Then, Year 7, I started at a brand new school and it changed. Kids had seen me on telly, and yelled out on the bus – like the character's name, Sally – and you'd turn around and they'd just snigger. I was a show-off little kid, but I didn't enjoy the attention. It's not a time in your life when you want to get singled out; it just heightened how unnerving it was to start out at a new school.

It's weird, that Year 7. It was lynchpin year for me. I went from feeling very confident in my own skin to very uncertain, which I think is a common experience. And I was at the mercy of teenage girls, who are the worst people in the world, ever.

There was a very tight-knit group of girls, Kristy, Leanne, and Wen Wen, who were the shitkickers of Year 7. Then there were three others – Lisa, who I'd known from primary school, me and Kathy – and it would rotate between us who was getting picked on. Every time it was me, it felt like a lifetime. There was no loyalty between any of us three, even though Lisa and I were really tight, because when it wasn't your turn, you absolutely tormented whoever it was.

And when it wasn't you, all you could think was, 'Thank f*** it isn't me. Yeah, Lisa does smell bad, doesn't she? Yeah, I want to put shit in Lisa's locker.' It's terrible to look back on it now, but there was such intense relief at having the spotlight taken off you for a brief moment. You believed that you were 'in' again, because Kristy had shone her light on you, and you were invited to slumber parties, and you got to pass notes about Lisa.

It's terrible to look back on it now, but there was such intense relief at having the spotlight taken off you for a brief moment. You believed that you were 'in' again...

I was horrified by that school. I really hated it. It was a private school that only went co-ed in 1978, so each class had about eight girls to 20 boys, and I had no choice about which girls I'd be friends with. It was so sports-obsessed, and I was terrible at it; for years I begged to leave and my parents kept going, 'It's character building, it's character building.' Eventually they let me leave, in Year 11, and the school I went to was total freedom. They say now they should have let me leave sooner; I was just so miserable.

Even in the 'off' periods, when I wasn't the one under the microscope, I lived my life on edge as this brittle lieutenant. Laughing at all Kristy's jokes, trying to get in good with Leanne, because I was thinking, 'I've got to ride this one out while it lasts.' I could hear the sound of my own voice, so shrill and false, trying to toady up to them – which they treated with disdain, and of course that made me feel worse. I'd hear myself in the back of my head going, 'Why am I doing this? She's not that interesting, why am I jumping through hoops to try and impress her?'

I'd come from primary school being a very bossy child – I know, it's hard to believe – and I'd organise lots of things along the line of, 'Okay we're going to rehearse at recess and lunchtime, put on a performance that I'm directing and starring in, and you can all be in it, and you have to say it strictly the way I say.' I tried to carry on that tradition in Year 7, in that show-offy way that girls do. I was 'in' at that point, we were very close, and Kristy and I did 'Time of My Life' from *Dirty Dancing* in front of the whole school assembly.

It was pretty much like *We Can Be Heroes*, I think, where Ja'mie and all the girls do a performance and there's lots of squealing and hair flicking. So then we were working towards doing *Starlight Express*, which was very topical at the time, and Kristy was going to be Pearl, the 'sexy' train. I was probably overbearing and bossy, but I thought my creative vision was the best way of doing things. Hey, that's how it had always been in primary school.

And it happened overnight. I went to school one day, and no one was talking to me. I walked up to my friends, and they just started snickering. And I said something, and they all turned and ignored me, and that feeling in your gut just drops, and it's, 'Oh, *shit*.'

They'd jammed something in my locker so I couldn't open it, and they started an 'I hate Marieke' petition, and this was years before the internet and commenting anonymously. They got people to sign it, and were flashing it around in front of me, and I remember really clearly sitting in the counsellor's office, because I couldn't, just couldn't, stop crying. I was physically unable to go to class. It was pure torment. I absolutely wanted to die. I was so sick my parents let me stay home for a couple of days.

They weren't any help though. They'd say, 'They're just jealous', or 'They're not your real friends', which was worthless. They just didn't get it. I can look back now and go, 'It's only Kristy. Her opinion doesn't matter. What the f*** is she ever going to grow up and do? Nothing.' But you can't say that to a 14 year old, because that's their entire world, and Kristy is the most important person in it, and if she doesn't like you, you are going to die.

Your world collapses and you never want to leave the house again. I still have those days. If I do something terrible, or hurt someone, I still think, 'I don't need friends, I don't think I'll ever see anyone again, but I'm okay with that.' And I convince myself that I'm fine with no friends, because I just don't want to go through the torture.

What made me vulnerable was my impenetrable confidence. I was an only child, I'd grown up with very supportive parents, on film sets, in a very adult world. I was intensely precocious and creative, and just wanted to make things and do it my way. So people wanted to take me down a peg or two, make sure I knew my place, because I certainly wasn't one of the cool, pretty girls. I had a very awkward fringe and body, and my clothes were never, ever right. My socks didn't scrunch properly, my skirt wasn't clean. I think they just wanted to say, 'Listen, I don't think you've got the right to be so confident.'

What liberated me in the end was getting in with the drama group... Drama kids don't care what anyone thinks of them, they're too busy playing theatresports.

Year 8 was another terrible year, trailing around after Kristy trying to ingratiate myself. What liberated me in the end was getting in with the drama group, doing *Man Of La Mancha*. Drama kids don't care what anyone thinks of them, they're too busy playing theatresports. I was very comfortable with plays and choreography, and loved the intense friendships you get when you do a show with someone. I got this intense feeling of relief, going, 'Wow, I actually don't give a shit what Kristy thinks.'

So, once I wasn't being pushed around by Kristy and Leanne anymore, it was like I wasn't going to be pushed around by my parents either. I turned into an absolute nightmare teenager. I was obviously finding a sense of self. No matter how much scope my parents gave me, I pushed further and further against them. I was in a hurry to learn all my lessons, and learn them all the wrong way, and my parents had to stand by and watch, wringing their hands from the sidelines. It was a really horrible time.

Mum says she brought me up to be a strong-willed, independent young woman, she just wasn't ready for how early I took that independence. She thought when I was 16 she'd allow me a glass of wine. She didn't expect me at 14 to be sneaking out the window and going around with older boys and hanging out with bands, starting my career as a rock'n'roll groupie. We physically fought a couple of times, *wrestled*, and we're not a violent household. I was a nightmare, the worst kind, for about four years. I still apologise every Mother's Day. I basically just take her up in a hot air balloon, cry and say sorry for about eight hours.

The regret we all have is that we didn't live under the same roof together for longer. I was 16, which isn't very old, you know. We made a deal, because I was so intolerable, that I lived out of home for Year 12. They paid my rent, but I had to finish high school. After that I just paid my own rent and stayed out of home. Now I wish I'd given them more time. It's sad. You can't go back, it's never the same.

But I'd got my confidence back, the kind you find when you set yourself a little bit left of centre. I'd moved out of home, fallen in love, all my friends were Goths, I'd taken drugs, dressed funny and listened to the Beastie Boys.

Then, at 19, the bullying started again when I began work as a story editor on a TV soap, and it was exactly like being 13 again.

There were three women in the office who made my life a f***ing nightmare. Same story again; I was full of confidence and they cut me down to size. They'd speak in very obvious code across the office about me, and do simple things like get everyone but me a cup of tea. They didn't invite me to script department dinners, belittled my ideas, talked over me.

They add up, all those little things, but when you sit down and tell your boyfriend or parents, they say, 'It's only a cup of tea.' They don't get it. I was thinking, 'Am I imagining this? Am I going crazy?' I knew I was being persecuted, but the complaints seemed so minor when I said them out loud.

I didn't want to go to work; exactly the same feeling as at school. I got shingles I was so stressed out. I eventually broke into this woman's inter-office email account, and saw the messages they sent to each other all day, about how stupid my clothes looked, how I was up myself, all this stuff. Horrible. It was as bad, if not worse, than high school, because these were grown-ups. I couldn't believe it. They should have known better.

But, yes, being bullied absolutely gave me qualities I didn't have when I was younger. I'm reluctant to say it's a necessary thing to go through, but up until Year 7 I'd only been around adults, who thought I was smart and funny and cute. I had to be taken to the real world where not everyone was going to think I was utterly charming. That was a good thing. I don't want to say I *needed* it, but it wasn't like I was going to cruise through the next 35 years with people going, 'Aren't you just a delight! I've got nothing! Tell us more of your funny stories!' I mean, the first time someone did say, 'I don't like the way you write', my whole world would've collapsed.

Eventually it gave me more empathy, too, although not in the 'kill or be killed' time of Year 7. I had to get out of the forest before I could start processing it and say sorry to Lisa and Kathy. Which I have. A lot. I'm not impervious to criticism, or being told to change, just not by people who I don't care about. I pay a lot of attention to my boyfriend, my parents and my friends.

In terms of my writing, I think it's helped. When you escape the bullying and think, 'f*** these people', and feel that liberation, there's a truth and a defiance that comes out of that. My sort of writing *is* to try and write what I feel and know, and find some truth in there. The more people pick on you, the more you go, 'Hang on...' and you find out who you don't want to be, and what you don't want to become.

It's meant I've had to be very brave. It prepared me for blogging, and blogging gave me the real, the ultimate, sealing over of the skin. I've got the hide of a rhino from doing that. Just from the feeding frenzy. My politics are important to me, and I once said I never wanted to have sex with anyone who voted Liberal. People were going, 'Oh, I'm going to go to a rally dressed up as a protester, and I'm going to rape her, and then halfway through I'm going to say, "Ha ha ha, I got into Marieke Hardy."' I mean, that's amazing. Then someone else said my great aunty killed herself because I was so untalented.

Eventually you go, there's nothing worse for anyone to say. I actually don't care any more, it all just blends in. I brush it off. It's bullying on a faceless level, but I'm grateful for it, because it's made me really strong and able to take criticism on the internet. That said, nothing prepares you for the vitriol the first time it happens. You're sitting, looking at comment after comment, going, 'What do you mean you wish I was raped?'

In some ways it's a shame, and in others it's just reality. But when young writers say, 'What can I do?', I still say 'blog'. You've got an instant audience, a community of people who you can read and be inspired by, and who can critique you. This is important too. If you give your piece to your best friend she probably won't say, 'You suck.'

I like the way I write. I'm not going to get tied up in knots because conservative bloggers don't like me. Of course they don't. I don't care for them either. I don't read their websites because life's too short. I can't understand why people think, 'I'm going to go to Marieke Hardy's article, and comment, and that will put her in her place.' Well I'm sorry, it doesn't.

I got a real sense of self out of being bullied. It's given me courage. Because I had to overcome knowing that if I was going to perform something, or do a reading, that Kristy and all of them would be sitting in the f***ing audience giggling. That's really useful in a career where you think, 'I'm going to put this piece of writing out there, and 8000 people on The Drum are going to call me a f***ing idiot.' Who cares? I'm going to do it anyway. ”

ADAM BOLAND

Adam Boland is a legend in Australian television. Until the end of 2010, when he quit after ten years as creator and executive producer of Channel 7's unassailably top-of-the-ratings breakfast program, *Sunrise*, his golden touch made him more important than the five food groups and oxygen. His career, whichever way you view it, glitters more extravagantly than a Swarovsky crystal tea service.

Redefining 'wunderkind', Adam began his rocket-driven trajectory to the top as a self-confessedly below-average newsreader at Radio 4BC in Brisbane. By 24 he had commercial television in a squirrel grip, and at the peak of his reign was producing 27 hours of television a week and had nine flatscreens mounted on the walls of his Sydney apartment. Interestingly, at 35, Adam has decided to wind back his commitments not because of his workload but because he is 'bored'. He's still consulting on *Sunrise* two days a week, and opening a Korean bathhouse with his partner.

From the outside *Sunrise* looks as formulaic as eggs and bacon, but Adam attributes its runaway success to his experiences as a child being bullied from pillar to post. Having a violent stepfather, and being shunted from school to school like a poorly addressed parcel, Adam grew up with little sense of trust or family. His only stability was watching television, and as an adult he set out to literally create a family for himself – and viewers – through *Sunrise*.

Being victimised has left Adam with empathy, a tremendous drive, a mixed bag of anxiety issues, respect for therapy, and a deep understanding that for many people, the radio and television genuinely *is* their friend.

"**The root of it is that I went** to 13 different schools – I think eight months was the longest I went anywhere – so simply from a logistical point of view I was always the odd one out. For example, debating groups would already be assigned by the time I arrived, so I couldn't even be part of the geeky groups. My parents were essentially nomads; my mum in particular had this need to keep moving, to find something more, which is fabulous unless you're a kid.

I didn't have anyone I could get advice from, or retreat to. It was very difficult. Mum did the best she could. She had me when she was very young, 17 or 18, and I came along by accident, the result of an encounter at a drive-in, in the vicious cycle that is housing commission life in the western suburbs of Sydney. To her credit, she'd seen her friends fall into heroin, and wanted to escape.

On the flipside, she didn't have a concrete plan, and the guy she shacked up with for a long time was a meat-head. His style of parenting was to throw me across a room if there was a stain left on a knife after washing it up. My bike had a puncture once, and I wheeled it home, which was apparently the wrong thing to do. Instead of just explaining, he pulled the bike tube out of the tyre and whipped me over the head with it.

There were plenty of times when I was physically injured at home. All types of things. I had broken arms that couldn't be explained, and because I was going from school to school, things went unchecked. I was very short back then. I shot up later, but I was never strong and my coordination is appalling, so that notion of defending myself didn't come naturally. And because I had a bully of a stepdad I was accustomed to being the victim. Going to school was almost time out from the stuff at home.

My mum reckons that she noticed certain bipolar behaviours in me when I was a teenager. I said, 'That's terrific. Shame you didn't notice your boyfriend bashing me at the same time.' I'm great with guilt, by the way, and she's well and truly paid for it in so many ways. She's like the world's best mum now, very supportive.

I found it incredibly hard to make friends, to fit in. On my second day at one school, a guy came up, pointed someone out, and said, 'Go up and say, "Hey, I hear your brother's cracked some skateboarding title", and congratulate him, he'll really appreciate it.' So I did, and the guy was incredibly upset, and everyone in the class was saying, 'Why would you say that?' And it turned out his brother had had an accident on a skateboard and wouldn't walk again.

And then … the reality was his brother *hadn't* had the accident, but the whole class had conspired to set me up. I found it really hard to recover from that, knowing everyone was against me. People told me, 'Just roll with the punches.' Really? How do you do that? A lot of work went into that joke.

It hurt more when I felt I was getting close to someone, and thinking, 'Yeah, I've got a friend', only for them to turn on me. I remember one time in Mackay, I was genuinely excited because I thought for the first time in a long time I had a friend. I called him at home just to talk about stuff, and we got the bus together in the morning.

Then a bunch of bullies from a grade above, who knew I was a new kid and tormented me as much as they could, asked my friend whether he was *with* me, as such. It felt a lot worse than being hit to the ground when he said, 'No', and joined in the taunting.

I was also struggling with my sexuality. I worked hard to overcome any notion that I was gay, because I didn't need to give people any added excuse to bully me. I knew being gay was bad, because when I was in Year 5 I came home and called a boy at school a 'spunk'. My stepdad was just furious with me, clipping me across the ears and saying, 'You'll never say that again. No little fag's going to live in this house.'

That hit home very harshly and I thought, 'Oh, okay, got it.' I only needed to be told once what pissed people off, because I actively tried to limit reasons for anyone to have a go at me, either at home or at school. There was a long list of things that I would minimise – just 'being in their face', or walking into a certain room, or eating a certain chocolate, or reading a particular magazine, or looking the wrong way at someone, or sitting in a bus stop when I should have been standing. Anything.

And you know what? I don't know how I was at sport, because I just didn't want to risk being bad. Because if I was bad I would never hear the end of it. More excuses for people to bully me. I was a grand conspirator at getting out of sport.

A remnant from that time is to always sit in the corner. We've all had 'stick-it' notes on our back, but I got it a lot, and I often got pushed to the ground as well. I realised, 'Hey, don't allow people to come up behind you.' So I was always the last to walk out of the classroom, I always took a few steps to my left so I wasn't in people's direct line of sight, and I tried as much as possible to sit in the back corner of a room. And that's lasted. When I'm in a restaurant I strive to get a corner table, and with friends I sit purposefully with my back to the wall, otherwise I feel very anxious.

With the 'stick-it' notes, it wasn't so much what was written on them, it was just the fact that they were *there*. It was not knowing what people were snickering about, and trying to laugh along with them because you want to be part of the joke, and then realising you *are* the joke. It was appalling. I'd walk into a toilet and see messages written about me on the wall, and have to rush out from class with dark pens to try and cover them up.

I had a brief respite when my stepbrother came to live with us for a while. He was three years older than me, and for a brief time we were at the same high school in North Queensland. He was my opposite: terrific at sport, totally shit at English and academia, looked great with beautiful blond hair, girls loved him, they wanted him in the cricket team, they wanted him in the rugby league team... He gave me loads of shit at home, but at school he basically levelled a couple of guys who were trying to rough me up, and all of a sudden I felt protected. Maybe we all need a defender.

I defended myself from the cruel world outside by entering my own little world, and I was very happy doing that. I found writing stories immensely enjoyable. I wasn't part of group activities, so I had to create my own fun. I think my mind is very active largely as a result of constantly needing to feed it during childhood.

I'd retreat to the library at little lunch and lunchtime. I felt safe there. I read a lot, and I started writing a lot, and that's how I set upon the journey of becoming a journalist. I credit those lonely periods with teaching me how to read and write outside of conventional schooling. I became a very prolific contributor to Letters to the Editor in newspapers up and down the Queensland coast from about the age of 11.

Seeing my name in print did enormous value to my ego. When you see that you suddenly think, 'Oh well, perhaps there's something worthy here after all', and that became a driver in many ways. And because I wanted to continuously see my name in print, I had to keep writing. That became my motivating force, and it was a direct relationship between sitting in the library, and seeing my work appear outside the school environment.

I didn't ask my parents for much growing up, but I did ask for a typewriter so I could continuously write

letters. Throughout late primary and ea
there wasn't a single television producer in
didn't know me, because I would insanely har
suggestions and questions, like, 'Why is this character being killed on *Home and Away*? Why don't you kill this person instead?' They put up with me, and even offered me work experience.

I wasn't that interested in the stars, I was interested in the producers, because they had the power. They were in the media, and I felt that's where I should be. There was one programmer at Channel Ten and I would long to get his letters. Maybe there was a gay thing at work there too? Who knows. I wanted to connect with whoever, ultimately, was calling the shots.

In Year 11 I went to school in Cairns; it was a school full of hippies and I was accepted from day one. I had an extraordinary sense of happiness and never wanted to leave. It was okay to be different, and that was a wonderful, wonderful time. In the space of a year, and to me this is extraordinary, I was elected school captain. In many ways, that changed my perception of what was possible.

I took my school out on strike because of our learning conditions; we were being taught in a couple of buildings that had been condemned, and I remember calling a press conference. It was exhilarating, learning how the media worked, and having kids following my lead. I discovered that one way to feel accepted is to lead, and that became a very powerful tool in my mind.

I was given a daily show on the local radio station, called *Teen Scene*. It gave me a persona, it gave me confidence. I used it to get kids involved in stuff and tell them they had a voice. *Sunrise* has been the grown-up version of that; it's a vehicle to give a voice to people who otherwise wouldn't have one.

The big thing that got me through everything was watching television. That's where I learned my social values.

Then my parents moved again, to Sydney, and I had to do an entirely different two-year syllabus in one year. It was awful and the complete opposite of acceptance. You were expected to wear a tie and ensure your fingernails were a certain size and, 'Why isn't your hair brushed down?' And it was all about rugby, and, oh god, have I just gone back in time? It was agonising, but I got through the year and got on with it. You just have to deal.

The big thing that got me through everything was watching television. That's where I learned my social values. Not from teachers or peers, because I was going to so many schools, and my mum was never there, and my stepdad? Social values? Please!

I got them from *A Country Practice*. I would watch it intently and think, 'Oh, *that's* what happens.' That show was my constancy. No matter which school I was at, wherever

I was in Australia, without fail they were there every Monday and Wednesday night. I asked my grandmother once to take me to Wandin Valley, and she did. I got my photo taken in front of the hospital, where the Muldoons lived, where Frank and Shirley Gilroy lived. What an experience! I remember feeling, 'This is where my family lives.' That's pretty weird.

To this day, if it's on, I will watch it. I produced a show for Channel 7 called *TV Turns 50*, a four-hour-long show with a multi-million dollar budget in the Star City Casino, and the ultimate moment was reuniting the original cast of *A Country Practice*. It got a standing ovation from the crowd, but for me I had on stage the people who had taught me about life, who had taught me right and wrong. They had been my friends.

I'm still a big believer in TV playing a part like that in people's lives. I created *Sunrise* with that in mind. The show engages, the on- and off-air teams share, and I firmly believe that's what powerful television should be about.

Building the *Sunrise* team was the ultimate payoff. It's absolutely a family, and that's no mistake. I built a family because I didn't have one. I surrounded myself with people who would be loyal and I would be loyal back. I looked for people who'd be turned away from other media organisations, people who'd had ups and downs and felt disengaged or disconnected.

It's made for a very strong team. People don't leave *Sunrise*, unlike other media groups. That is immensely satisfying. I go to a lot of industry events and I still feel slightly intimidated – I look for that position in the corner – but when I walk into *Sunrise*, I feel relaxed. I feel totally at home with people who I love. That's a tremendous feeling and something we should all strive for.

We created something called 'The Sunrise Family' with our viewers, and we now have 220,000 members. Two full-time staff spend every day writing back and forth to them. On a big day we get up to 8000 emails. I wish I'd had the opportunity to talk to a TV show like that when I was a kid. We've had kids write to us who've been contemplating suicide, who we've been able to help. We're their *A Country Practice*. That's really, really gratifying.

I got a reputation very early on at Channel 7 for making enemies. I didn't care, because having had to fly solo for so many years, keeping people on side wasn't important to me. I would crash through anyone I perceived as being in my way, and I didn't worry about the ramifications. It was perceived as immense arrogance, and I understand why, although I don't think it was as simple as that. It certainly made me effective; you look back and think, 'Gee whiz, it worked, didn't it?'

I had a meteoric rise, but at what price? By the time I turned 30 I started to slow down and think, 'Whoa, whoa, whoa!' I was compiling lists of people who I didn't like, because they were standing in my way. What the hell was that? That's just nasty, man, and became the stuff of folklore within the TV industry in Sydney. But at the time it definitely helped me professionally.

Showbiz and entertainment can be just as awful as the schoolyard in many ways, and it took me a little while to realise that. I thought people only wanted to know me because of what was on my business card. I found myself dealing with depression while keeping a mainstream daily show on air. It's taken a long time to reconcile the things that happened in childhood, but I think I'm in a pretty secure position now. The message here is that if you've been through whatever hardships, particularly early, at some point *process* it. Otherwise they'll keep kicking at the back of your mind.

I've been going to counselling for years, and was diagnosed with bipolar about five years ago, and I've learned that I have a heavy dependence on friends now as a result of not having anyone to depend on when I was young. I have a limited inner circle, and I would trust them with my life. I take them with me from job to job, and I'm uncomfortable when they're not around.

I don't want to sound all American about it – you know, everyone needs a therapist – but it shouldn't be something we're ashamed about. The reality is anyone who thinks you aren't the product of experience is a fool. Our individual lives are a lot more complicated than what happens on Summer Bay. Why do we go to a GP for our physical body, but shun going to a therapist for our minds? The mind can do many, many dangerous things, and I'm a big believer in counselling. Blokes refuse to talk to their mates about what they're thinking. Why? *Why?* We all have complex thoughts; ask a mate, deal with them.

I went on Facebook a while ago, and tracked down maybe the top two or three bullies, and made little comparisons in my head of where I was at compared to them. I don't know what that says about me, but it *was* extremely satisfying. I don't still hold resentment towards them, but I do towards my stepdad, because he should have known better.

I feel sorry for some of them, because it's very easy to join the bully crowd. I get that. Everyone wants to be accepted – it's human nature to want to be in the cool crowd. And if the way to do that is to make other people feel unaccepted, then that's what happens. I did it myself later in school because I felt, 'Oh yeah, I'm on that side of the fence now', but that's a shocking place to be.

I firmly believe what happens to you in childhood does have a lasting effect. I think my career is a direct result of what I went through, and I've got a lot to thank my childhood for. At the same time I have a lot of anxiety, and an inability to trust people at times. But it's helped me to be more defensive in some aspects of my life. I'm a lot more streetwise than I would have been, and I have a level of empathy I might not have had.

I think I've had a terrific life but was it the best childhood? No, but would I necessarily have been as successful without it? I suspect not. I doubt I would have gone on this course without those experiences. I wouldn't have become a journalist, I wouldn't have done plenty of things. You have to go through those periods to get there, but the light at the end of the tunnel is always a nice prospect. ”

BINDI COLE

If art were as celebrated in Australia as, say, sport or beer, you'd have already heard of Bindi Cole, a photographic artist who's rising faster and harder than a death metal guitar solo.

She gained attention and notoriety in 2008 with her solo exhibition *Not Really Aboriginal*, which included images of her extended family made up with minstrel-era blackface. Since then she won the $25,000 Deadly Art Award, had five major exhibitions, and in 2011, with eight other fair-skinned Aboriginals, she sued *Herald Sun* columnist Andrew Bolt under the Racial Discrimination Act.

Bindi's heritage partly explains why her award-winning work delves so deeply into identity and belonging; being of English, Jewish and Wathaurong descent gives her plenty to play with. But for Bindi, who scraped to the end of year 11, it's also because she found school as bad a fit as her unironed uniform. With unsympathetic teachers, a fractured home life, and neglect masquerading as freedom, Bindi has spent much of her life isolated, and wondering what it means to belong.

What makes Bindi's art so striking is that it's playful, empathetic and fearless. There *might* be a topic she's not prepared to tackle, but due to her childhood her comfort zone is so far beyond 'normal' most of us couldn't spot it with a telescope. Her artwork has been included in some school syllabuses, which strikes Bindi as both ironic and delightful.

“**I never finished high school.** I got to year 11, which I ended up finishing by correspondence. I sent some stuff in, but I think they gave it to me because they felt sorry for me. It was the year my mum passed away from bone cancer, and I couldn’t face going back to school after that. My world had been turned upside down and I was essentially on my own, so I started to work instead, and earn money.

I’d ended up at a school in St Kilda, which was full of the naughty kids that had been kicked out of other schools, whose parents were at the end of their ropes essentially. You could smoke and swear, and we were put into groups that would sit around and talk about ‘values’. We had classes, too, but they felt kind’ve tacked on. It was more about teaching us how to function in the world, to be part of society.

I have to say, it mainly helped me to be naughty. I was naughty before, but being there really solidified it. I didn’t start off that way. My nan would tell you, when I was little all I wanted was to be a good girl, and I would try to do the right thing and be nice, but over the years I realised I could get more attention … in other ways. But, then, that school was where my mum had really wanted me to go; she’d never wanted me to go anywhere else.

I was sent there after getting kicked out of a public school that operates like a private school; it’s academically advanced. Thousands of girls and boys from all over Australia and Asia apply to get in, and they take 120 for each year. My nan wanted me to apply, and she was so proud when I got in. I lasted one year. I just didn't fit in; I wagged classes and ended up graffitiing the school.

I was bullied there, but not by students. By a teacher, actually. I came from a home where, well, there was no nurturing of me in relation to my physical needs. Everything I needed, I did myself. We were very working-class – at that point Mum was writing and earning a little money, but before that I'd come from full-on poverty. I was 14, 15, and I was in charge of maintaining and looking after my uniform. I must have been a sight; my mum also had nine cats, so I would have been covered head to toe in cat fur. I wasn't the most polished student, I guess.

So I'd turn up to school and the headmistress would pull me aside, regularly, and lay into me, tell me that I didn't belong at that school, I didn't scrub up enough, my uniform wasn't ironed, I shouldn't be there. It was nothing to do with how I was doing academically, it was how I looked, but there was really nothing I could do about it. At 14, who cares? I didn't care about my uniform. I just stuck it on every day. Mostly parents care about that stuff, I suppose, but my mum didn't care about it either.

What a horrible woman that teacher was. I'll never forget her. She was so awful to me. It's interesting, a case of bullying from someone older, but that's what it was. She didn't offer me any support, which would have been the way to go, actually, because it was never a case of me not being bright enough to be there. She didn't bother to find out why things were the way they were, that no one was looking after me. All she did was give me a hard time.

It made me so angry, and it hurt. So I acted up. I'd wag a lot, and I'd make myself stand out more. I graffitied my school shoes with bright pink polka dots, which, no, wasn't school regulation. And I would shorten my skirt. I don't think, actually, that I was trying to rebel. I wanted to fit in, I just didn't have the capability at that point to physically be what they wanted.

I didn't have any boundaries. At all. It makes school a lot more difficult. It makes life more difficult, actually, because you have to learn them later.

I was quite isolated, I think, looking back. I had friends, but they weren't from school, they were the daughters of Mum's friends, who were also probably junkies, people like that. I didn't get on well with the other students. I had a lot more freedom because I didn't have curfews. I could go out and party all night, and I didn't have any boundaries. At all. It makes school a lot more difficult. It makes life more difficult, actually, because you have to learn them later.

My situation was pretty unique, even in primary school. Mum never made me lunch, but if she had it she'd give me $5 and I'd walk up Fitzroy Street to St Kilda Park Primary, stop at the milk bar and buy a peanut butter roll and a Big M. If she didn't have that $5 I didn't go to school. So I always had a lot of time off school, one or two days a week. School never seemed valuable, because if there wasn't $5, I didn't go. It's difficult, too, I suppose at that early age, to make friendships if you're not always there, and you're the feral kid.

The problem wasn't that I lived alone with a single mother, it was that she was a stripper and a drug addict and a prostitute. And so … she wasn't really there, and I saw things that people probably shouldn't see. When I wasn't at school she'd take me to work with her. Mum danced at the Shaft Cinema for a few years, so I'd hang with her and the other women out the back. When it was Mum's turn to dance, in between movies, to keep me safe she'd put me up in the projection booth. So, I was seven or eight, and I'd see the end of the movie, and then I'd do the spotlight for my mum while she stripped.

I remember telling the teachers at primary school, and being pulled aside, and me saying, 'Yeah, yeah I do the spotlight for my mum, stripping on stage.' I had counselling from then on, which I loved because I didn't have to do maths. I remember thinking the counsellors were so dumb, because they asked me the stupidest questions. They'd ask, 'This colour is black, what emotion does this make you think of?', and I remember knowing I was telling them what they wanted to hear – 'Black makes me angry, and pink makes me happy' – and that I was manipulating them as a little girl.

I was always a bit of a loner, I was never part of the popular group. But because I was being singled out a little by the teachers because of my home life, the other girls started to gang up on me. They made up poems about me, and would come out at playtime and skip around me singing the poems, which would often end in 'Bindi Cole the moll.' Little kids are excellent at rhyming, aren't they?

This went on for a while. I remember it made me upset, but mostly mad. One girl was teasing me at playtime, so I walked up and punched her in the head. And she went *running* to the teacher, I remember this so clearly. 'Bindi hit me, Bindi hit me', and the teacher said, 'Well, you shouldn't be teasing her', and I was like, 'Yeees!' Because I really hit her hard in the head. It wasn't the first or the last time I hit someone for being mean.

Of course, I saw a lot of violence growing up. I saw my mum being hit. People using drugs – heroin, mostly. Smoking bongs, cigarettes, that was just everyday for me, normal. You think that's just what life is. I remember police stations when I was young, and being in dealer's houses.

Dealer's houses seemed like mansions to me, because they were always new and nice, and we lived in tiny one-bedroom flats in St Kilda. One time when I was, gosh, I must have been about six, sitting there in this lounge room with my mum, waiting for her to score. And *Flesh*

Gordon was on the television. And there's me and Mum, in this posh house, watching *Flesh Gordon*, and laughing at the robots with the pointy boobs.

I wasn't invited to other people's houses, or sleepovers, or parties – I think I was invited to one friend's birthday party the whole time in primary school. I certainly never had anyone over to my place. I was very much on the outside at school; in hindsight I guess I really wasn't very popular. I did know some local kids in the neighbourhood, because I spent most of my childhood just kind've hanging out by myself in the St Kilda Adventure Playground. I never strived to be part of a popular group, it never drove me, but I never understood why I wasn't. 'Cause I just thought I was all right, you know? But I was probably a bit feral.

I still think I'm a loner. I struggle a bit reaching out to people. I'm just used to operating independently, because when I'd get home from school, I wouldn't have friends there and Mum would be out of it. And when I'd wake up in the morning Mum wouldn't get up. I just spent a lot of time on my own as a child.

I simply didn't have a strong family supporting me, or any decent foundation, so I'd get into trouble. My mother was very good in a lot of ways. I knew that she loved me through all of this. I mean, even when I was growing up I loved photography, and Mum bought me cameras and a developing tank. I'd take photographs and develop them in my bedroom. She was weird like that. She couldn't give me lunch, but at Christmas she'd spoil the crap out of me. It wasn't that I lacked love, I don't think, it was just that she couldn't look after me and she couldn't look after herself.

My experience is that it's not intelligence, or anything else, that makes kids act up, it's the kids who don't have a strong family behind them. So, if you're starting off life without that, you're really starting off on the back foot, and you miss out on being given a sense of self-worth.

Once I didn't go back to school at 16, I was essentially on my own. I met a boy, same age as me, and we got into a relationship for four years. I was isolated anyway, but I became totally isolated. He was very abusive, hit me, and destroyed things of my mum's, things that I loved. We were taking drugs together and drinking, self-medicating. I was living with him and his mother, and she was kind of cold, but she helped me out. She saw me working at Hungry Jack's, how I'd get up and go to work no matter what, and she bought me office clothes, taught me to do my make-up, and got me a job as a receptionist. By the time I left him I was working at Pricewaterhouse. I don't know where it came from, but somehow I've always had a good work ethic.

My next really great plan was to go overseas, isolate myself even more, and self-medicate over there. Brilliant. I had a complete meltdown in London: everything went out of control and I just … imploded. I became very, very sick, a full-blown addict. Which was interesting, because I'd thought I wasn't like Mum at all! Because I used other drugs, never heroin, you see...

When she'd died, I'd thought, 'I don't want to be anything like her.' She was creative, so I thought I'd do exactly the opposite and be a really hard worker in the corporate world. Realising I was just like her enabled me to begin to deal with things, and explore my creativity.

I would absolutely not be the artist I am now if it weren't for what I went through in childhood. If you can allow it, those experiences strengthen you. It makes my work richer, for sure.

When I was arrested and locked up for selling drugs, I was 42kg. So skinny, so sick. I'm sure I was about to die. I'd overdosed about three times. I'd isolated myself so hard, and run so hard, so fast, that I ended up locked in a tiny cell on the other side of the world at death's door. I'd hit that rock bottom people talk about.

I was in prison for two years, long enough to change your life, and it did. From the very second I was put in that cell, a spiritual peace descended on me, and it's never left me. I knew I was in the right place, and that things would change for the better. At my core, I wasn't alone anymore, and that really gave me strength. The world would consider me religious, but I think there's a difference between what I am and religion: I think I have a relationship with God. As an artist I've begun exploring that more, and the show I curated at the 2010 Melbourne International Arts Festival was about spirituality. We're all searching for something.

The other important thing was watching Mum turn her life around in her last few years. That was her biggest legacy to me, to show that it's possible to pick yourself up and make a go of it. Ultimately I had to do that too. She wrote about her experiences, and in her final years was accepted into Melbourne Uni, published in *Meanjin*, and became writer-in-residence with the Melbourne Workers Theatre.

I would absolutely not be the artist I am now if it weren't for what I went through in childhood. If you can allow it, those experiences strengthen you. It makes my work richer, for sure.

Because I've never really felt like I belong, and spent so many years reconciling my identity, I find myself interrogating identity and belonging in my art. I always identified as being Aboriginal, and as I got older I realised that I didn't fit the stereotypical notion of what an Aboriginal person is assumed to be. That was hard. Hilariously, I wasn't teased at school for being Aboriginal, because I looked white. A bit of a mongrel, really, is what I think I am.

My work's about identity because of things in the world, such as the attitude of people like Andrew Bolt, that made me uncomfortable. Rather than turning away from it, I explored it. Making that art, and as a result having Bolt attack me for not looking Aboriginal enough, and getting up in court and defending myself, has only strengthened me. I have a strong sense of who I am now; that discomfort has gone.

Going to court was very empowering. My past was disempowering, and I'm so thankful I've had the opportunity to stand up for myself. Another thing is I don't have any bad feelings towards Bolt. I'm not sitting here hating on him, or resenting him. I feel a little sorry for him; I feel sad because I think he's got something wrong with him, that he needs to walk over people. I've had to do a lot of forgiving in my life, and it's given me back my power. I don't feel like a victim, myself, at all.

Being someone who was always on the outside allows me to sit in that space as an artist very comfortably. Until I started making art I didn't realise I saw things from the outside. I certainly didn't realise that people would be interested in how I see things; that still blows my mind. But I realise I can look at something uncomfortable, even if it causes me discomfort, and be okay with that, and make a story out of it. Being uncomfortable, for me, is just normal.

The background I've had makes it easier for me to be 'brave' as an artist. There's not much that I could see, or could be done to me, that could throw me these days. I don't feel like I need to belong to the mainstream, and

I don't feel like I need to connect to things that other people might need to validate themselves.

The other good thing is I think I can live without a sense of security. As an artist that's very valuable. I don't need money in the bank, I don't mind living day by day, which enables me to be freelance. I don't need what most people need. I can take more risks, because I can go for periods where I'm struggling a bit and it's okay. I have a very strong sense of, 'I'll just get through stuff, and it'll be fine.' It's been a really, really hard journey, extreme actually, but now things are good. Bring it on.

I guess I'm a bit of a late bloomer. I only really became comfortable in my skin in my late twenties. Personally, I don't think schools are designed for people like me, where I was at in my life. School is the middle road. It's really easy to slip through the cracks at school, and be left out, be isolated, if you don't fit in.

But I got value out of going to university. I always wanted to go, it was my dream before Mum got sick. But all these things kept coming between me and that dream. Years later, when I really wanted to learn photography, I decided I *would* go to university. I applied to lots of courses, and I was knocked back from everything except one TAFE course, and I did that two-year diploma and it was really, really good. It gave me the technical base that I needed. After that I had a few exhibitions, and *then* I got into uni.

But now I get invited to speak at all the universities I got knocked back from, which is hilarious. And a few years ago they included one of my photographs in the Year 12 art exam; they had to write an essay on my artwork, which was also hilarious, because I never did Year 12. That's a nice little full circle thing. ”

CHARLIE PICKERING

Middle-class, white, intelligent, confident, from a stable home, on the hockey team, not ugly, and yet, somehow, Charlie Pickering still managed to be duffed up on a regular basis. His private school days are a grand reminder that just because you fit in, it's no guarantee that you won't be singled out like a limping gazelle on a savanna.

Ultimately, being targeted has worked to Charlie's advantage, giving him a strong social conscience and the determination to pursue happiness. A comedian who turned his back on a career in law, Melbourne-based Charlie did the hard yards in stand-up and emerged as one of Australia's most visible television talents; he's the Generation X Team Captain on Channel Ten's *Talkin' 'Bout Your Generation*, and co-host of *The 7pm Project*.

Charlie's career is going off like a Mardi Gras dance party. His first book, *Impractical Jokes*, was published in 2010 and his first DVD, *Live at the Time of Recording*, was released in March 2011. He considers that being bullied has prepared him well for life in the public eye; hostile tweets from disenchanted viewers are water off a duck's back when you spent your high school years antagonising bullies then ducking.

"**I went to an all-boys private school,** and it had a strong anti-bullying policy. They were very much on about it in assembly, saying often that bullying would not be tolerated and would be punished. They'd go into detail about how physical bullying is bad, but psychological bullying is worse, so you don't have to be beating someone up to be bullying them. Bullying was discussed and it was understood. But it didn't stop it from happening.

For me, bullying took a few forms. I was smaller than everyone else; I skipped a grade so I was almost a year younger. I was a late physical bloomer, I wasn't the kid that out of nowhere hit puberty like a freight train and all of a sudden had muscles and a beard. I was never that kid. I still can't put on muscle really. I wasn't big, and so I'd get physically intimidated by people, and I would be bullied by the guys who were always the big dumb jocks that went and did weights at lunchtime.

There was a definite hierarchy, with jocks at the top, nerds at the bottom, and everyone else in the middle. The most important thing was rowing. We were always made aware that the rowers were working very hard for the glory of the school. They train so much, they get up so early and they work so hard, so we all have to pull together and show some support for the rowers.

That in itself fed this culture that the biggest and strongest were at the top of the chain, and the smallest and weakest were at the bottom. The great irony of it was that every mid and end-of term, everyone got an academic ranking, with the Top Five for each year published in the school newsletter that went out on the Friday afternoon. There was this sudden highlighting of academic achievement in a very competitive way, so everyone had to care about their marks, and if you were the kind of person who studied a lot instead of lifting weights, it was your time to shine.

When I started there in Year 8 I didn't know what rankings were; my previous school hadn't done that. After a semester I came in at number 40 (out of 123), and I'm a very competitive person, so I was like, 'I'm sure I could do better than *that*.' I got my name in that newsletter relatively quickly, once I knew that there were rankings. Like I said, I'm competitive.

If you made the Top Five it was seen as an achievement, and the teachers would say 'Well done', but generally in the playground and around the school it didn't mean you were on level-pegging with the Captain of the Football Team, or the Captain of Boats, the Stroke of the First Eight Rowing Side. Yeah, yeah, I went to school in England in the 1800s.

I *was* very good at hockey. I was actually in the first hockey team for three years. But that's not a cool sport to be good at. You know, like, on the food chain of sports, that's well down the list.

The bullying happened in Years 9, 10 and 11. I'd get pushed around, physically intimidated, tripped over, shoved into walls. There was a guy in my basketball team, Sam, and he'd throw the ball at my head. From behind. We were on the same team, so you'd think you'd be okay, but he was very aggressive towards me. I'd get duffed up between classes, because that's when we were unsupervised. It wasn't all the time, it would come and go. There'd be periods where I was targeted, and then they'd mess with me at every opportunity. It wasn't the physical aspect so much as never knowing when they were going to be there. I was always on edge.

Kind of the worst was when someone would be threatening me throughout the day with the idea of an impending beating after school, and so I'd go through the whole day thinking I was going to have the shit beaten out of me. I'd be thinking, how can I get from roll call, out of the school and home, so that I can escape this? That's just awful, the psychological side of it. I think the teachers were right; it is the worst. It's much worse than the physical side; a beating is never as bad as you think it's *going* to be.

I'd just get teased and picked on. I had a smart sense of humour and was quick with the comebacks, but that would escalate what was going on. It was a blessing and a curse – I had a weapon and a defence mechanism, but it often got me in trouble. The problem with having a comeback is you have the ability to make the bully look small in front of his friends, because they've inevitably said something really dumb to give you shit. And that's when they escalate to violence. I've had guys say, 'Right, you're f***ed', jump over a table and throw me to the ground because I said something that cut them down to size.

The advantage, I guess, to the anti-bullying policy, was that when I would get bullied I knew it was wrong. At no point did I think I was bringing it on myself. But it doesn't mean you can do anything about it. I mean, the last thing you're going to go and do is dob a bully in to the headmaster. You feel that's only going to make it worse.

The idea of physical supremacy in a school hierarchy is celebrated everywhere. It's how it is. I was sort of in the middle. I wasn't one of the nerds, hiding in the library at lunchtime, but I wasn't one of the bigger, tougher athletes or in the cool group either. The middle was a good place to be, I thought. My group of friends all found the same stuff funny, and the most important thing was our sense of humour. I was lucky to have that group around so I never felt entirely alone. That said, when the bullying happened I'd feel instantly alone. It doesn't matter who you're friends with because it's one person picking on you directly and you feel threatened and intimidated, and it's an instantly solitary experience.

There wasn't an undercurrent of racism, as far as I know. The Asian students hung out together in what was called 'Chinatown' but no one was pulling their eyes at the side and putting on bad Mickey Rooney accents. There was actually a sense of curiosity; they had cool gadgets and were the first to get mobile phones. We thought they were from the future. I don't recall economic prejudice either. We lived in a very affluent suburb, and it was an affluent school. The scholarship kid was good at footy, so you weren't going to pick on him. There were academic scholarships, but they'd be picked on for being geeks over being on a scholarship. But kids did get bullied, and it shows that even in a wealthy private school, where you take away real financial disparity between people, people will still find a reason to pick on someone. It's like water finding the lowest point.

The best way to disempower a bully is to not care about the bullying. It takes away their reason for doing it, if they're just like a fly buzzing around an elephant.

I don't *really* know why people picked on me. Maybe I bit back just enough to draw attention. I never hesitated putting my hand up in class. I didn't hold back or try to make a small target out of myself, and I was a class clown and a bit of smart-arse. But I didn't throw up any major red flags on a bullying profile. I wasn't any of the usual laundry list of arsehole reasons to pick on somebody for something completely beyond their control. I wasn't poor, fat, gay, black, stinky, asthmatic, particularly uncoordinated or disabled. Maybe that was part of the point: there wasn't a particular reason.

There's always going to be bullying, I think. It's part of nature – big strong shit eats the small weak shit. But as much as it seems when you're in high school that the big, good-looking, stronger, faster kids are going to rule the world forever, it levels out in time.

It could be very hard, and sometimes I had to lie to everyone to give off the air that I didn't care. It took some acting sometimes. But I reckon the best way to disempower a bully is to not care about the bullying. It takes away their reason for doing it, if they're just like a fly buzzing around an elephant.

I never let it damage my self-esteem. There were days when I felt shitty, or threatened, or intimidated, and I would wish I was bigger and stronger and could do something about it, but at no point did I take it on board and think, 'Maybe I deserve this? Maybe I am this shit.'

I've never gone to a psychologist to talk about when I was bullied; I don't feel I need to. I'm happy, but maybe there is something that has seeped in. The idea that you should always try to make the right thing happen. Not right for you, just the right thing. I guess that's an overarching goal.

Being bullied definitely affected my political outlook. It's really given me a sense that governments shouldn't be there to serve the strongest and richest; governments should be there to serve the weakest and poorest. I don't like bullies in any form and I will always, always take the side of the victim in a bullying situation. That's the flipside of bullying – you should always stick up for those who have no one to stick up for them.

I'm not intimidated by anyone, either. It doesn't matter who I meet. Okay, sometimes I might get giddy because, I mean, like I met Lou Reed and I was a little bit, 'Holy shit, I'm in the same room as Lou Reed', but I wasn't intimidated. That's good and bad; early on in my current career it may have been interpreted as arrogance. It wasn't even confidence. It was just, 'I won't let myself be intimidated.'

I think, actually, that being bullied made me more resourceful; I have the idea that if things are hard I know I can dig a little bit deeper to get through something. Nothing is so bad that I'm not going to get through it. I've got a pattern of learned behaviour, which is, 'Something shit happened to me and I got through it, and things are okay.'

I was well into history, and that helped. I would often go, 'People survived proper hard stuff, why should I get to feel bad?' Being picked on by the big kid is nowhere near as bad as war, or death camps, or starving on the streets of India or Africa. Learning about it [proper suffering] made it really clear that my bad day was nowhere near as bad as the best day of someone else. Heaps of people have a much worse day than you.

It also made me determined to not be unhappy. I studied law, but I'm not a lawyer, because it was *never* going to make me happy. I love the law, I'm fascinated by it, but I started work in a law firm and in my first week I looked at the guys in the corner offices. The senior partners – who, in the realm of the law were considered very successful – were 40kg overweight, didn't really know their wives, barely remembered the names of their kids and couldn't remember the last time they had a holiday.

I want to succeed in whatever I do, but I just looked at them and thought, 'If this is success then it's not for me.' So I burned that bridge, rolled that dice, and I went back to what I wanted to do since I was ten, and that was to be a comedian. It didn't pay off straight away; it took a really long time. And all my lawyer friends have made a lot more money than I have. But it's taken its toll; they're all bald and look way older.

To me it boils down to 'Why not?' Like, why *not* be one of the people who wins? Like, if you've got a choice, if your choice is between winning and losing, why not try for winning? You can do nothing and lose. Anyone can lose. Why not have a crack at winning, what's the worst that can happen? If you lose then, at least you know you didn't lose because you didn't try. In my mind I think undeserving people win all the time. So why not try? It's amazing what you can do when you tell yourself that you can do it.

In terms of my work, the advantage to having been bullied is I don't let the haters get to me. I get cyber-bullied – there are things written on websites about me that are horrific – but I'm old enough to know that it is utterly meaningless. If it crossed into the real world and someone came after me physically, that's different. But in a grown-up realm there are laws against that shit.

What people say about me doesn't bother me, it never will. I mean, this happens: people will say on Twitter that they want me killed. They genuinely say that they would like me to be killed. But if you listen to everyone who has something nasty to say about you, you'd never get anything done, you'd be a wreck. I'm not letting that damage my self-confidence. Who cares? Who cares what people say?

In the end it's all meaningless. Who gives a f*** what a bully thinks? Who gives a shit what some idiot at school thinks? You're going to agree and disagree with thousands of people in your lifetime, so why let one get through to you?

When I look back at the kids that bullied me, I reckon they had shitty parents. My guess is they had a pretty crap time at home, and they were taking it out on someone else. But I have no sympathy for them. I'm sorry they had a shitty house to go home to, but that's not my fault, lots of people have problems, and they don't take it out on someone who doesn't deserve it.

The thing is, high school is formative, but it's a tiny part of your life, and every year that goes by you realise it more and more. None of it is there forever, and it becomes a very small part of your life. By the time you're 22 you think the 16-year-old you was a bit of a dick. By the time you're 25 you think the 22-year-old you was a bit of a dick. By the time you're 30, if you look at the 16-year-old you, you'll say, 'What *were* you thinking?' ❞

KATE MILLER-HEIDKE

It's possible to imagine Kate Miller-Heidke not fitting in, even though she's blonde, luminous, gifted and grew up in Queensland. Her platinum-selling, idiosyncratic songwriting tells the story, pointing to that deadly schoolyard double whammy of weapons-grade quirk and emotional sensitivity.

Being an odd little unit made school challenging for Kate, but her *eclecticism* has worked wonders as an adult. She trained in opera and won many awards as a classical singer, but eventually she chose to focus on pop and writing her own material. It's likely she found Gilbert and Sullivan limiting, given that her most popular song on YouTube is 'Are You F***ing Kidding Me?', a viral hit about an obnoxious ex trying to 'friend' her on Facebook.

Most of Kate's music packs an emotional punch, something she attributes directly to experiencing ten types of misery at school. Her song about bullying, co-written with husband Keir Nuttall, 'Caught in the Crowd', won the US$25,000 Grand Prize in the International Songwriting Competition in 2008, and reached thousands of kids through a video-making competition organised by the NSW Department of Education.

She starred as Baby Jane in *Jerry Springer: The Opera*, has been nominated for no less than eight ARIA awards, and approaching 30 her career is tracking better than an Olympic shooter – it's probably just as well then that Kate Miller-Heidke didn't try too hard to fit in at school.

"**You know you look at a Grade 1 kid**, and they're only five years old? And they look so tiny and innocent? Yet it's so important for kids to rank themselves in some kind of social structure. Within the first week of Grade 1 at primary school I was acutely aware of the social hierarchy that was going on. By week two or so I'd ranked every kid in my grade from one to 100, in terms of their popularity and status. And … I was about the fourth least popular. There were a couple of kids who had learning difficulties so I always had one up on them.

I was really sensitive, and aware of it. But at the same time I couldn't modify my own behaviour, so I couldn't figure out a way into this intricate system. The reason I graded everyone was because I was near the bottom. If you're up high there's no need. They do say that the happiest people in life are the loud, ignorant ones, and those who are quiet and introspective struggle.

The schools I went to were mainly, I guess, upper middle-class. The criteria for being popular, or at least socially acceptable, were being good at sport, having symmetrical features, and not having any opinion that others might deem as weird. I was shit at sport, and really eccentric. In Grade 3 I announced to my class I was going to become a stripper when I grew up, and that pretty much destroyed my social life for the rest of primary school. I was about eight, and I don't know where I got that from. Luckily I kind of raised my standards as I grew up.

I just didn't fit in with the other kids. At the same time as being highly sensitive, I was socially weird. I still am. I had a complete paralysing insecurity coupled with completely irrational confidence, and that turned people off. I was bullied all through primary school, and through to Grades 8 and 9 in high school.

When it came to sport I was picked last for every team, and you know how you had to line up and hold hands in groups of two outside the classroom? Nobody wanted to hold my hand. It sounds pitiful and stupid now, but I found it terrifying, because I knew I would end up at the back of the line by myself. That's a big thing when you're a kid.

At the same time as being highly sensitive, I was socially weird. I still am. I had a complete paralysing insecurity coupled with completely irrational confidence, and that turned people off.

I always felt like an outsider. I've got two brothers, but even though my younger brother was at the same schools, he was too young to be an ally. So I really felt isolated, and I couldn't talk to my parents about it because it seemed so trivial and insignificant. They can't get on the wavelength of a small child, and how devastating it is to be socially rejected when you're six or seven years old. I always remember that feeling, that I couldn't tell them because they'd just say, 'Oh, get over it', or 'It doesn't matter.'

At high school I'd go sit in a toilet cubicle through morning tea, and all of lunchtime, so I didn't have to see anyone. There were very good acoustics in there, so I'd sing, but I'd stop if anyone came in, and wait till it was empty. I'm sure that did a lot for my reputation: 'That crazy bitch is in the toilets again.'

There was a boy who used to prick me with safety pins all through maths in Grade 8, and there was one girl who took a big dislike to me, and every time I'd see her – anywhere in the school – she would run up and give me a dead leg, or a dead arm, and scream insults at me and stuff. Then one day in Grade 9 she just punched me in the face.

That was that, and I changed schools. I had a great excuse to leave in that my father had just become principal; obviously it becomes worse when your dad's principal. Both my parents are teachers, and all in all I changed school six times in primary school, because they got posted around different places in regional North Queensland.

I did try and fit in. In Grades 8 and 9 I observed some of my popular classmates from a distance – obviously they wouldn't let me too near them – but I saw how they acted, and how they spoke, and when I changed schools in Grade 10 I did an incredibly accurate impersonation of a popular kid.

It was very successful, and I was at the top of the social hierarchy for the year. Then I changed schools again because they wouldn't let me do both music and drama, and at the new school I just couldn't be bothered keeping up the charade because it was too tiring. I settled back into where I belonged.

The first friends I made were in the children's chorus of a couple of amateur musicals up in Brisbane, because everybody was the reject from their school. That was a great outlet.

I was in the chorus for *Oliver* twice, and I still know people from then. Most of them are extremely successful now.

Things ease up for everybody around Grade 11, I reckon. I became friends with the smokers and the musicians, and, yeah, we were the weird kids. I was happy with that. I felt that was my place. I had good friends for the first time in my life, and they were all artistic in some way. There weren't many, but enough. I think as long as you've got three or four friends in life you're okay.

What's great about getting older is the pressure to fit in morphs and changes into an appreciation for people who are different, and almost an admiration. I know *I* love strange people. Most of my friends are very eccentric, some of them highly eccentric, and I like those sort of people, I find them interesting.

The isolation of school can be extreme. You're surrounded by people all the time, and yet it's the loneliest place in the world if you don't fit in. But I'm grateful for it now, because it made me retreat into music, into my own brain. Being an outsider is useful, because at the heart of good songwriting is the ability to observe. That's the key: to observe, and articulate an experience in a new way.

What I've taken from being bullied is there's this little knob of self-hatred that comes in handy when it comes to being able to self-examine and self-criticise. Particularly in terms of doing drafts of your work, and knowing what to cut and to keep. It means I'm being constantly challenged to do better, and create better things, because whatever I create I still hate myself to a degree. It's a spur; maybe the next thing will help me like myself a bit more.

I'm driven by that feeling that nothing's ever good enough. There's no room for complacency. It's a useful feeling for an artist: that everything I've done in the past is shit and I have to do better next time. I'm never satisfied. And, as an artist, having a nice big well of pain and insecurity to draw on always helps. Having feelings of isolation and rejection can be handy songwriting tools. I wrote 'Caught in the Crowd' inspired by that time, and it's my favourite song off the album *Curiouser.* It resonates deeply with me, and I get a lot of young people mentioning it, saying the song helped them in some way. I'm so glad about that.

I think if you've been happy your whole life you probably don't have much to say as a songwriter. It was hard at the time, but I know for sure that I wouldn't be doing what I'm doing now, had not every element been in place – the kind of child I was, the kind of people that were at my schools. Everything has led up to this point and I don't regret any of it.

It's made me stronger; I don't feel defeated at the first hurdle. I feel like nothing's ever come easily. And doing music as a career you get a hundred setbacks for every one small success, so that's probably been useful. In that sense I'm psychologically adapted to being an artist, but that's not to say I don't have self-doubt. But I think everyone in the arts experiences that friction between complete arrogance and total self-loathing, and it's where those two overlap that great art can be made.

I feel self-sufficient as a person. I'm pretty independent and fairly resilient. As a musician you have to deal with bad reviews and people's negative opinions of what you do, and I feel like I've had a bit of practice with that. One legacy is that it's hard for me to collaborate. I collaborate with my husband [Keir Nuttall], but it took a long time to be able to trust and open up. I haven't done much with other people; I've tried and it's been quite awkward, so it's something I'd like to work at.

It's a cliché, I know, but I honestly do think being bullied was character building. Because it was impossible to express myself socially, I was basically forced to withdraw into my own head, my own imagination, and often just live in a fantasy world. I was inherently a creative child, and I'm appreciative that I had that outlet. It's nice to be good at one thing when you're a kid.

I always loved dancing, singing, musical theatre and generally making a fool of myself. That was what consoled me and comforted me growing up. I used to spend five or six hours a day in my room playing my guitar, writing songs and listening to music. I was actually really miserable, but I wouldn't swap it for anything. I'm glad, now, because I do think it leads to a much richer inner life.

I think most intelligent people at some stage in their lives have to withdraw. If you just float along in a sea of good looks and popularity all your life, and never truly have to examine what it means to be a human, well, you don't end up being an artist. One of the definite advantages of being unpopular is that you are actually forced to examine yourself. ”

'Caught in the Crowd'
Songwriters: Kate Miller-Heidke; Keir Nuttall.

There was a guy at my school when I was in high school
We'd ride side by side in the morning on our bicycles
Never even spoken or faced each other
But on the last hill we'd race each other

When we reached the racks, we'd each go our own way
I wasn't in his classes, I didn't know his name
When we finally got to speak, he just stared at his feet
And mumbled a sentence that ended with James

I was young and caught in the crowd
I didn't know then what I know now
I was dumb and I was proud and I'm sorry

If I could go back, do it again
I'd be someone you could call friend
Please, please believe that I'm sorry

Well, he was quite a big guy, kinda shy and quiet
When the kids called him weird, he didn't try to deny it
Every lunchtime he'd spend walking by himself
'Round the boundary of the grounds 'til he heard the bell

Well, one day I found him, joined him on his walk
We were silent for a while until we started to talk
I told him my family were fighting in court
He said his step-dad and him always fought

We talked about music, he was into punk
Told me all the bands that I liked were junk
I said I'd never heard the songs the Sex Pistols sang
I laughed back at him and then the bell rang

I was young and caught in the crowd
I didn't know then what I know now
I was dumb and I was proud and I'm sorry

If I could go back, do it again
I'd be someone you could call friend
Please, please believe that I'm sorry

It was after school in the afternoon
The corridors were crowded as we came out of the rooms
Three guys I knew pushed him into the cement
Threw away his bag and said he had no friends

He yelled that he did and he looked around
Tried getting up but they pushed him on down
That's when he saw me, called out my name
And I turned my back and just walked away
Yeah, I turned my back and just walked away

I was young and caught in the crowd
I didn't know then what I know now
I was dumb and I was proud and I'm sorry

If I could go back, do it again
I'd be someone you could call friend
Please, please believe that I'm sorry
Please, please believe that I'm sorry

TIM FERGUSON

If you had to nominate someone who was indubitably, unquestionably, categorically not bullied, it would surely be Tim Ferguson, aka the 'pretty' one from cult Australian musical comedy trio, The Doug Anthony Allstars. For a heady decade (late 80s, early 90s), Paul McDermott, Richard Fidler and Timothy Dawson Langbene Ferguson terrorised audiences with their devastatingly addictive brand of belligerent music-based humour. They were daring, brilliant, aggressively sexual and exhibited all the vulnerability of a Sherman tank.

And yet Tim was serially bulled at school. Tim's difficulty was partly that he was a skinny noob with a sharp wit and posh accent who sucked at sport, but mostly that he was always, always the new kid. He attended nine schools across NSW and the ACT and put down fewer roots than a plastic pot plant. He approached school as a life or death game, always searching for strategies to get him through.

The weapon of choice was his scalpel-sharp sense of humour, which Tim has used throughout his life to sculpt a brilliant career. A performer, writer, film-maker and television host, he's also – not by coincidence – a highly popular sessional lecturer in Screenwriting and Writing TV Comedy at the Royal Melbourne Institute of Technology.

Tim's trust in his big brain turned out to be a good call; his sports-shy body revealed itself to be unreliable when he was diagnosed with 'repeating and remitting' multiple sclerosis in 1995. The unpredictable physical legacy of MS meant the demise of the Allstars, and a lifetime of reinvention – something he was particularly well-equipped for by having to survive a parade of schools.

“**My dad was a journo** [Vietnam war correspondent Tony Ferguson], and my parents just kept moving around. All in all I went to nine schools, which meant I was always the new kid. I never had any status, I never had any ‘hand’. It was like every 18 months or two years, picking up and moving on; even if we moved back to the same place, I’d be in a different school. My brothers were too far ahead and behind me for there to be fraternal support, although I took care of my younger brother when I could.

I was punched at every school I went to. Being skinny and smart, well, that’s immediately daunting to the guys with big frames; they don’t like to think because it might lead to them expressing themselves. The only weapon I ever had was my sense of humour – it was the only thing I could use, because humour is aggression by other means.

So, the first of it was at a Sydney school, year three or four, and there was a guy who just didn’t like me. Maybe I’d cracked a joke at him or something, I don’t know, but he decided that I was no good. So he took to giving me regular thumps. One time he thumped me, and I fell over, a teacher saw us, and we were both accused of fighting. I got the cane. I was nine. And, seriously, if I hadn’t been looking up with big tear-filled eyes as I held my hand out to be whipped, I would have been whipped harder. I wasn’t turning it on – I was terrified. I thought, ‘This is no good.’ I told my dad and he said, ‘Oh well, just thump him’, but the guy was huge. And I’m not really a thumper. I’ve always been slight. So I had to let it roll on until the glorious day that we moved, and I left the school. But at the next, in Bathurst, it was much the same thing, a couple of guys who thought I talked funny.

They reckon the worst thing about having a stalker isn't when the stalker is actually there, it's in the coming home every day and wondering if they're in the house. The fact that they're not doesn't make you any happier. It's the same with a school bully.

I've got this sort of colonial 'days of the Raj' English accent from when I was in Singapore. I was there for the first six years of my life, at the time when you learn how to talk. My brothers shook it off, my parents don't have it, but I just got lumbered. It makes people think that I'm smarter than I actually am, but that's just the cap-doffing Australian way.

They reckon the worst thing about having a stalker isn't when the stalker is actually there, it's in the coming home every day and wondering if they're in the house. The fact that they're not doesn't make you any happier. It's the same with a school bully. Even if today isn't the day he comes up and says, 'You, me', and thumps you, you spend all day, every day nervous, with a vague sense of dread.

High school turned out to be even worse, because one of the schools I went to was football-obsessed, and I wasn't big on catching and kicking. Or running. And that became a problem for the other guys on the rugby team, because I had to be included – it was compulsory.

So they put me on the wing, because they figured that by the time it had been passed from one person to the next to the next to the next, someone else would have taken care of it. The low point was when I heard someone yell, 'Don't give it to Ferg.' That's when I knew, these guys weren't really on my team. The coach came up with a wonderful solution, that I was put 'in the reserves', and a kid was brought up from another year to fill my role. Which was actually good, because the people watching the game were the girls, who'd turn up to see the boys. So I'd sit talking to the girls through the match, while the boys were out there trying to kill each other and look heterosexual. It's actually far more heterosexual to sit and talk to women rather than run around trying to grapple with men's arses.

That was not an argument I could use off the field.

The thing is, you're just an outsider – I wasn't on the team, I was excluded. There was a lot of verbal bullying, exclusion and accusations of homosexuality. You're definitely gay if you read books, because everybody knows that reading leads to sodomy… In fact, the only time I could talk to girls was when all the guys were occupied trying to kill each other. Once the guys were off the field, well, you know teenage girls, they weren't talking to me. They like brutal idiots. They always like brutal idiots. Why? Because brutal idiots could save them in the jungle when we were all still apes.

So, you know, the downside to all this was it began to give me a dim view of everyone around me. Because I thought, well, the girls must be as stupid as the guys if they think they're going to do anything except sleep with them, throw them away, and move on to the next one. To keep myself sane I hung around with the other nerds, and made jokes about those guys.

I even got bullied at free school [Canberra-based School Without Walls]. There was one guy, he was my friend, and he'd been thumping me in a kind of friendly way. But I was 16 and I'd just been thumped enough. I turned to him and said, 'Don't hit me or we can't be friends', and he didn't ever again. It was quite a moment. Like anything that's hard, we've got two choices. One is to let it beat us, the other is to follow Nietzsche and say, 'It's going to make me stronger in some fashion.' And it does. Even the decision alone gives you petrol in the tank.

I was full of trepidation every time I moved schools, always in a heightened state of alertness, because when you're moving into a new, established group of people, you have to work out what the status mix is, and where your place is in it, very quickly – because if you're completely isolated even the nerds won't talk to you. I made a point of ingratiating myself with as high status a nerd as I could find, because there's no point hanging around with the Epsilons, because then you're trash.

There was no point in engaging because I was never around long enough. School was just about trying to make them laugh and get by without being hit. After a while I worked out that the *really* good people to talk to at school were the teachers. They had the power. And I think the teachers knew the deal, why I was around at lunch. Because, of course, if you're talking to a teacher at lunchtime, no one's going to screw with you. From Year 7 onwards I did that at every school: knock on their door, have a question to ask them, and the next thing you know an hour's gone by and that was lunch.

The thing about ostracism, and not fitting in, is I developed the skills to generate my own world. You can't be in the *actual* world, so you make a little fake one. I didn't engage emotionally at any school, because I knew I was going to leave, but I became extremely good at making everybody else feel like it was the real thing. I learned how to motivate and inspire people, and make them feel like they're in the centre of the world, by doing it again and again at different schools. I'd talk to the people who other people wouldn't talk to, and say, 'We're the smart ones! They're the idiots! And we're going to rule the world.'

But loneliness comes with independence. And most of the time, when you're lonely, you don't realise that you're lonely, because there's always someone in your head, which is you. But the inability to speak to someone other than yourself can really become very frustrating, to not have people who can match or understand or help you in any way. It's very isolating, so you retreat into yourself, and that makes it even worse. It becomes self-fulfilling.

But I ended up having a wider range of skills and tools through not being what I was, which was fun. One tool was to read a lot, because it's you and the author and the imaginary world. I read more and more as I got older. It's a useful escape. But eventually we have to learn to balance escapism with action in the real world, otherwise you just end up an academic.

The other thing I did was to assemble two or three people around me who were influenced easily enough to go along with whatever personality I was portraying that day. So, effectively, I developed the ability to do pretty much whatever I wanted at the next school. I had the skills to be whatever someone seemed to want, to be just about anybody. If they were a quiet person, then I too would become a quiet person, and we would understand each other. And if they were gregarious, I'd become like that, match them, so that they'd feel they were living the right life and being the right kind of person. I tended to be whatever was required at the time. I took on various guises. The hopeless romantic, the super-smart comedy tough guy, they were all just different masks. But at the heart of it is a lie. It's not who you are. It's fawning to the person you're dealing with.

It also means that I became very compartmentalised. You can't be one person, a shy person, and a gregarious person at the same time. So I would keep people and worlds separate, so I could be a different person here, and a different person there. Which is no way to live. It was very clinical. I was a sociopath, effectively, just not one that kills people. One that gets along. I was a psychopathic get-alongerer.

I've figured out now I have to be myself, and they either like me or they don't. So I'm the same annoying, opinionated guy pretty well everywhere. And people tend to like that. It took me a long time to decide – and it was a decision – to assemble lifelong friends, because I'd never been given a chance to assemble those people. I'd had to develop friends quickly in high school, and as an adult I realised that they couldn't have been that good friends because I would leave a school and throw a lit match behind me and never think of them again.

Once school finished, I never wanted to go again. The idea of university I found incredibly daunting, because I thought it was going to be more of the same. I'd seen university students. There were guys with beards who drove cars, and I just thought, no, never, I can't be institutionalised again. So, no, I didn't go to uni, but I sound and speak as though I did. Everyone thinks I did, even in the media, but no. In effect I got my degree when I was four years old, in Singapore, when someone said, 'No, we pronounce it *dahnce*.'

I was very lonely. Oh yeah. But that's what makes us who we are. There are good things that have come from being bullied, in the sense that it changes the way that you're built. The DNA of my personality was forged by fear, and that's the most powerful motivator. There's desire, but when you're a teenager that's just, 'Please, can I just see *one* set of tits?' But fear, that can create some of the best things for you – the mechanisms we devise for protecting ourselves from the thing we're worried about.

It made me a comedian, because I found just naturally, not consciously, that comedy was the way to get to the top of the tree. When you're a comedian, even the biggest footballer in the room has no power. You've got him by the goolies as soon as he's bought the ticket. I liked that immediately. Hey, who were we [The Doug Anthony Allstars]? We were the most aggressive act ever, and Paul and I were both bullied.

The other thing I gained is the ability to lead people. To keep them inspired and convince them of new ways of doing what they're doing, in a way that makes them not feel that they're being treated like an idiot, but that they're being given the opportunity to change, to shed a skin. As a skin-shedding specialist from my youth, I find it quite a natural process to help other people do that.

Teaching has been a revelation to me, a gift, because it's placed me in the position where people want to know what I know. And knowledge transforms people. I love that feeling that you're not just telling people things, but empowering them, changing the way that they think, broadening their world and giving them information on how to be funny. And comedy, it's a regenerative act in that it gets people thinking, and it can be used to attack and tear down the biggest lions in the paddock. I talk about the school bullies quite often, and use them as examples of comic characters.

I have a determination to succeed. I'm at a point in my life now where nothing can hurt me, in the sense that nothing can really get in the way of me doing the things I need to. Like making this film [*Circle Work* was in development]. It doesn't matter what the roadblocks are, the film will get made. Or I will kill people. In a sense it's the empowering act of having to create yourself due to the dim view others have of you. People don't like you and you can't work out why. Well, it gives you a way to give people a reason why.

They say depression isn't sadness, it's unresolved anger. In a way, being a comedian is the perfect release for that, the perfect neutraliser. I went to a therapist once, after three years in the Channel Nine grinder, because I thought, 'This is bad.' And I went to this 75-year-old one-eyed woman, and told her my whole life story, and it was just fabulous. It was her who said that having gone to so many schools was a problem. She said, 'Of course, you're depressed', which I'd never thought about because I was angry. I always thought depression was just having the sads, and I'd never had the sads, I had the dark mutters. And that was a revelation.

It's interesting. A lot of people want to be famous because they want to be recognised in nightclubs, or they just want the money, or to be on the front page of a magazine. But I realised, a long time after I'd been famous for a while, that there was only one thing driving it – I didn't ever again want to go into a room and have people not know me. I never wanted to be the new kid again. ❞

PENNY WONG

Politics isn't easy. The hours are gruelling, everyone hates you, and there's more back-biting, bitching and bickering than backstage at *Australia's Next Top Model*. No matter what your views on Penny Wong's politics or policies, it's impossible not to be impressed by her grace under pressure – the Federal Minister for Finance and Deregulation is so cool, calm and collected she'd be a shoo-in as the next James Bond if she could just make with the one-liners.

Penny's bulletproof demeanour is essential in a frequently hostile work environment, where she sticks out like a pork chop at a vegetarian barbeque. In the homogenous sea of mostly middle-aged white guys, she's not only a woman, but the first Asian-born Federal Senator, and the first member of the Federal Cabinet to be openly gay.

It will come as no shock that Penny started honing her 'sticks and stones' armoury at primary school. Born in Malaysia, Penny moved to the Adelaide Hills when her parents broke up, and her Australian mum, Jane, returned home. Penny and younger brother Toby were the first Asians that anyone in 1970s suburban Adelaide had clapped eyes on, and they were received as a cross between an exotic sideshow and a sci-fi film called *Aliens Attack*.

Penny pretended not to care, studied assiduously to compensate, and developed a hard-won understanding of discrimination. Her path became even more challenging when Toby took his own life in 2001. Penny, who found her way to politics through law, and as an industrial officer with the Construction, Forestry, Mining and Energy Union, says that one of her prime motivations is to battle prejudice and change people's attitudes for the better.

“**Primary school was a real shock** to the system. I had bad migraines for a couple of years, and my mum took me to the doctors to check my eyes and stuff, because they were so bad I'd get double vision. I've never had anything like it since, and I suspect it was the stress of moving to Adelaide, not living with my father any more, leaving the home and culture I knew, and coming to this cold place where people had a go at me.

School was, I'd have to say, a pretty difficult time in my life and in my family's lives. I don't want to overstate it, because we had parents who loved us, and food on the table, and there are many kids who have a harder life than that. But we did cop a fair bit about our race at school, and from one of the neighbours who just – she just had a problem. It varied from people who asked questions because we were new and different, to people who were obviously prejudiced.

I came to Australia in 1977, when I was eight, and we lived in the Adelaide Hills. The community wasn't very culturally diverse, and my brother and I were the first Asians that I know of. We were certainly the first people of Asian background to go to that school.

The school I went to in Malaysia was completely different. It was diverse, very multicultural. It was an international school, and had kids from every background you could imagine; there were lots of British, Australian and Canadian expats, and kids from the local community whose parents wanted an English-based education, so lots of Indians, Chinese and Malay.

When we went to get enrolled at school in Adelaide, my mum and I walked across the asphalt, through the schoolyard, and the children literally formed a path around us and on either side, and commented on me. They were saying, 'What is she?', and someone said, 'She's Hong Kong-ese', and I'm thinking, 'There's no such thing, what are they talking about?' I realised for the first time that my race was something that people would notice, that it was an issue.

It was all about race. My sexuality wasn't an issue at school, because it wasn't formative. It was much later in my life that I entered a relationship with a woman. I get it a bit now, though!

It was all about race. My sexuality wasn't an issue at school, because it wasn't formative. It was much later in my life that I entered a relationship with a woman. I get it a bit now, though!

I never like to talk about some of the things I remember. I'm not sure if it's because it brings back how it felt to hear it, or whether it's because I don't like to repeat words of hate. It's hard to talk about, and it's very hard to talk about my brother. I think he probably had fewer defences than I did. People are born differently, and I suppose he was more vulnerable and gentle, which is a beautiful thing, but it's harder in the world.

I dealt with it by trying not to respond. I tried to ignore it, and not show if it hurt. It was, 'I'm never going to let you see, in any way, that this gets to me. I'm never going to let you see that I feel upset, or lonely, or shy.'

And I also did it by trying to be better than the people who were teasing me, so I have no doubt I became much more focused on studying, getting good marks, doing well on the sporting field, those sorts of things. I decided I was going to be better than them, and achieve in this field, and this field, and this field.

I was trying to prove that I could succeed no matter what they said to me, and no matter what they thought of me. That I could do well no matter what they threw at me. It wasn't so much to get people to like me, to become my friend; it was that I wasn't going to allow them to keep me down. My reaction was to want to get better marks in the test, or do well in the relay or pool.

I didn't become insular. I've seen that happen with kids, but that wasn't my response. I just pretended to be confident, even when I wasn't. I learned to be steady and still, even when it felt very messy and difficult. You know, to hold yourself steady, even if your reactions are really strong and your emotions confused.

It wasn't easy. It got better as time went on. I learned a lot. I learned how to rise above things, or at least pretend that I was. I also found that for most people – not all, but for *most* people – prejudice doesn't survive personal relationship. Sometimes it would come out in different ways: 'We don't like Asians, but you're okay', which I always thought was kind of funny. But sometimes children say things and you can't blame them, because they're just repeating what they hear around the table at home.

My mum was a lot of support. She would come up with one-liners of varying degrees of utility. I think she found it very hard to have her children targeted, and to be essentially powerless to stop it. Like all you can do is love them and support them, and try and help them with strategies to handle it, but ultimately they've got to go out and handle it themselves. That was very hard for her.

And look, I was lucky. Mum's from a family of five girls, and my aunts were really good, particularly Ally. She was great, incredibly loving and incredibly supportive, and the attitude was, 'Don't let them get to you, they're not worth it.' So I drew a lot of strength from my family.

I suppose in hindsight, I have learned a lot from school. It taught me you have to try and turn the things that life throws at you to good. You know, use negative experiences, and make the best of them, because sometimes you can learn from them in ways that do help you later.

I found high school a lot easier than primary school. When I went to Scotch College, I found there was a lot less racism. The teachers there were more supportive, and there were more things I could do, so I was able to engage more.

But, you know, because of my experiences at school, I know what it's like to be different, and to be targeted because of it, and it probably influenced my decision to go into politics. I'm sure you can trace that desire in me to change things for the better to my childhood. If I hadn't gone into politics I would have done something else consistent with those beliefs.

Interestingly, I've certainly not lived a life where I've avoided monocultures. In fact, if you look at the choices I've made around career, I've put myself into environments that were not particularly diverse at all, you know, whether it was the trade union movement or legal work or Parliament.

In the end, politics isn't that different from the schoolyard.

When I entered Parliament, there was me, Senator Tsebin Tchen from Victoria, and at that stage Michael Johnson may or may not have been in the Parliament – his mother was from Hong Kong – and there was the woman who worked in the library. In this huge building, that was it, apart from, you know, the cleaners. There are Greek and Italian MPs today, from the more settled communities, but we still don't have a Parliament that's as diverse as the Australian community.

I have no doubt it's easier for me to navigate through that environment because of my school experience, because the hardest part of it is how you think about it internally, how you manage it inside you. I know I started to learn how to do that at school. In the end, politics isn't that different from the schoolyard.

I absolutely learned pretty early on how things that are wrong can become accepted, and how important it is to stand against them. I still react when there are issues of race, where I think the other side are toying with the sorts of prejudices we know do exist. I do react, and there is a personal basis to that.

For people like me, racial discrimination is not an abstract principle, it's about our lives. And I haven't lived the hardest life – I'm the Minister for Finance and it's an extraordinary and privileged life in many ways – but when you talk about prejudice or discrimination to someone like me, it's different than to someone who's had no experience of it.

It's much less now – I think Australia's a very different place from what it was like in the 1970s and early 80s. But on occasion, someone will still abuse me in the street, or something else, and whenever I've told my friends, they're surprised it happens.

I once read a comment by an Aboriginal woman – I can't recall who it was – where she talked about the concept of parallel universes here in Australia. She said, 'The Australia I live in is not the one you live in; when I walk along the street, or when I go somewhere, how I'm seen and how I'm treated, is a different world to yours.'

I remember thinking, 'I understand some part of that.' Not *as* much, because I think Aboriginal Australians have had the most sustained level of discrimination of any group in our society. But my experience of what it was like to be in this country was very different even from people who were close to me. Because they just couldn't comprehend that people would be like that, whereas I knew they could.

It's so important for political leaders and politicians to stand up on issues of prejudice, even if they're not personally affected, because it's about the sorts of values and ethics you're backing in the community. It's the easiest thing in the world to speak to people's fears, and it's the wrong thing to do. The positions we hold shouldn't be used like that.

I try and bring the values I have, and the ethics in which I believe, to the job. They include a view about equality, and I was part of the pushing for the affirmative action changes inside the party. I think that people can be better, less willing to turn on others, more open-hearted and more open-minded. That's a belief I've brought to my political life.

Part of why I've always been completely open about my relationship [with Sophie Allouache], if not interested in having a long discussion about the detail of it, is I just thought it was important to normalise it publicly. To say, 'This neither makes me less, nor more, qualified to do what I'm doing.' Being open about it was a statement in itself, I think. Normalising being different is important, because being different is okay.

I thought it was really interesting, the difference between my first swearing in and the second. For the first swearing in they photographed Sophie and Mum and it gets on the front page of the papers and people comment about it, right? The first time a same-sex partner goes to a ministerial swearing in! The second time, not even commented on, not even a photo. I thought that was fantastic, like that's a really good indication of a step being taken.

I think, 'What do we aspire to?' One of the things I aspire to is a nation in which we genuinely are judged – and succeed or not – on the basis of our abilities and our character, and not on our attributes. Not on where we were born, or where we went to school, or how wealthy our parents are, or whether we're gay or straight or white or not. That's where we should always be walking towards. ”

BENJAMIN LAW

The most important requirement for writerly success, apart from knowing where to stick an apostrophe, is having something to write about. For Benjamin Law, a Brisbane-based memoirist who is compared flatteringly to David Sedaris more regularly than Tom Cruise appears on the cover of *Scientology Monthly*, sourcing material is a snip.

Benjamin grew up a runty kid in a large, broken family, dealing with being Asian on the then whiter-than-white Gold Coast. He survived school by exhaustively camouflaging his homosexuality behind a complex smokescreen of walking straight, talking straight, acting straight and loudly insisting that he wanted to shag Buffy the Vampire Slayer.

His first book, *The Family Law*, is a collection of rich and hilarious essays about his extravagantly eccentric family. His second, *Gaysia*, will be a travelogue based throughout South-East Asia, where Ben has travelled to visit various gay, lesbian and transgender communities in countries less queer-tolerant than Australia.

As an essayist, Ben's very conscious of writing for the next generation of misfits – given that he was gasping for something that normalised difference when he was at school, and convinced that every move he made screamed 'GAY' like a homophobic air-raid siren. He's also a senior contributor to *frankie* magazine, and has written for *The Monthly*, *The Big Issue*, *ABC Unleashed* and *The Courier Mail*.

“ **I had every reason to be picked on** at school. I was really scrawny in primary school, exactly one head size – like a human skull – shorter than my classmates. I was pretty much the only Asian kid in my year level, I didn’t play sport, and was just really into reading. I should have been mercilessly bullied. But, for some reason, my classmates thought I was a cool novelty. I had a shaved head, so it felt like a soft toilet brush, and they’d rub it for luck. I had a quick wit, and the oldest students basically saw me as a mascot, barely human, more like a cartoon character really.

There were two main reasons I think I was never figured out as gay in school. One was that I’m Asian, and people can only handle a certain amount of minorities in one person. For me to be Asian *and* gay would have been taking it too far. I slipped under the radar.

The other is, when I hit puberty, my balls must have dropped like anvils or something. I suddenly developed this super-deep, baritone voice. So there was this runty, skinny Asian guy walking around sounding like James Earl Jones. I didn’t have the ‘voice’ that a lot of people associate with gay guys.

It was the 90s, and probably the last few years where it was social suicide to come out at school. I basically knew I was gay throughout high school, maybe even before, but it was impossible to talk about what ‘gay’ was because it was the worst thing you could be. You couldn’t talk about it without completely ostracising yourself.

At a young age, when kids aren't into gender roles, you can get away with more. At primary school I was sort of prancing around, and playing jump rope with the girls. I gradually became aware that if I was hanging around the girls too much it was seen as odd. If I said, say, I liked the TV show *Man O Man*, then I'd be told, 'Nah, you can't talk about that show. Why are you watching that?'

You don't want to be gay, right? If everyone in the schoolyard, and on television, is telling you that being gay is one of the most embarrassing, horrific things you could be? It's a hideous prospect. You don't want that! I was incredibly ashamed, because gays were the freaks, and the only gays you saw were when the Mardi Gras came on, and to all your friends, and even to you, they looked like an absolute freak show.

And if there's one thing that kids and teenagers are very, very efficient and good at, it's being able to smell out any sort of gayness or difference – even before the other kid knows they are gay or different. People would get up at assembly, and they'd have a slightly gay voice, and everyone would crack up laughing. Or people would call each other 'lesbo' or 'homo' or 'fag' or whatever, when someone was acting 'gay', or liked drama too much.

So you find ways of, at the very least, not acting like that. My strategy was to hide it. Not talking about it became important. You know, they say gay people are very good actors, and you have to be to survive. You see the kids who can't hide it, and how they get picked on, so I examined them and did the opposite of what they did. It was pretty dark. I watched other guys, and how they acted, and copied them. I'd see myself walking in a glass reflection, and think, 'Oh, okay, I need to take longer strides, because that's how manly men walk.'

I became super-conscious about what I wore. 'Do these pants reveal that I'm gay?'

I stopped doing gymnastics as well. For one thing it was really intensely physically painful, but it was also a prissy thing that you just rule out. I had some good friends, but I felt very cut off as a teenager. There's a level of self-consciousness that you carry constantly, a gnawing little monkey on your shoulder. It was suffocating. I questioned myself all the time, making sure I didn't emphasise the fagginess of liking books and drama.

I remember giving a Valentine's Day card to a girl who I thought *maybe* I liked. I knew I liked guys, but I thought maybe I could like girls as well. You try, but it feels wrong and strange. It just lands you in trouble, because they ask you if you like them online, and you end up fumbling and closing the window, saying goodbye really awkwardly.

You adapt. Playing a role wasn't something I consciously thought about. It's like a reflex. If the other guys are into Sarah Michelle Gellar, and think she is a babe, you pick that up straight away and start talking about Sarah Michelle Gellar as a babe. You have to put on a bit of a show, present to be someone you're not. I think most kids have to develop a playground persona, and for gay kids it's a lot more pronounced. Particularly in high school, when everyone talks about who they want to f***, who they've got a crush on, and 'Did you see those tits on TV last night?' You use that vocabulary. There's a bit of bogan in me that I can switch on if I need to. I can bogan it up.

The thing that came naturally to me, which wasn't much of an act, was to be gross and disgusting. I still like to make foul jokes, and I'm obsessed with disgusting stuff, and since this is typical macho behaviour it helped me be part of the gang. I emphasised the things people liked: jokes and stories about farts and poo.

Weirdly, I liked school, probably because my home life was hard. When I was 12 my parents split up, and Mum became a single mother of five children. That was huge. It was a really dramatic thing for all us kids, and it made for a really tough environment. We saw Dad less and less, and the discussions at home were very stressful and claustrophobic. We were always looking for escape, and I really enjoyed getting up, going to school, and getting the hell out of home.

I think all teenagers have shame about something ... body shape, acne, their family, their grades. When you come down to it, shame *is* the singular teenage experience. Because I was *really* different, a lot of my energies were extended towards trying to iron out the differences and fit in.

I found my family shameful as well, because it was – what's a nice way to put it? – difficult, and hard to function within. There was nothing shiny or glamorous about my home. I went to a quite rich private school, it was co-ed Lutheran. Hardcore. Daily devotion. I'd go to my friends' houses, and their parents had functional relationships, and their crockery matched, and their Christmas tree had a singular aesthetic rather than looking like a bomb hit it. All those things made me very self-conscious and ashamed. But, yeah, being gay was the main one.

I made up my mind to come out at 17, just after school had finished, and before I went to university. One of the things my parents instilled in me was whenever the opportunity presented, just take it. Going to university was a big deal for me. Not only had I never left home, but I'd lived in the same house my entire life. Starting university represented a lot of freedoms – I was going to be making brand new friends, and I didn't want to have to hide. I didn't want to have to play games and pretend that I found Sarah Michelle Gellar really hot and wanted to stick my dick in her. I didn't want to have that conversation any more, because it is tedious and exhausting. Telling people you are gay when you meet them is exhausting enough, but it is far more tiring having a fake conversation. I'm too lazy, in the end.

Coming out is one of the most horrific things that binds gay and lesbians or transgender kids together. You're a young person who has never been able to talk about a very fundamental secret your entire life, and you have to vocalise something in your brain that has never been said out loud. It's incredibly frightening.

I came out first to my best friend, Rebecca, and I just could not stop crying, because the fear when you're revealing yourself for the very first time is completely mortifying. She was great about it. Then I told my mum. I was really emotional and scared, and I couldn't say the word and I made her guess what was wrong.

'Are you on drugs?'

'No.'

'Have you got Rebecca pregnant?'

'No.'

'Well are you gay?'

'Yes.'

Then she said one of the most f***ed up things you can say, and one of the most brilliantly consoling things you can hear as well – 'Don't be silly. There's nothing wrong with being gay. Something went wrong in the womb, that's all.'

A few friends said they suspected, because I was really into drama and arts and books, despite growing up on the Gold Coast where everyone is sporty or a surfie. My siblings were all surprised, but then you watch home videos of, you know, ridiculous fashion parades, and they start shaking their head and think, 'How did we not know?'

One by-product, I guess, of the double life, is that I learned how to please people, and make sure they see what they want to see. You know that you don't fit in, so you sort of force yourself to fit in. You find a way of making people like you. It's a stereotype, but a lot of gay men are funny, right, and I think humour is a way of getting people on side. I could make people laugh, and that took attention away from the fact that, for instance, I liked guys.

One by-product, I guess, of the double life, is that I learned how to please people, and make sure they see what they want to see.

I made jokes, and hey, sometimes those jokes were gay jokes, which is weird when you think back on it. The sad thing is, I watched kids known to be gay who were picked on, and that meant you avoided them as if your life depended on it, because if you associated with them you copped flak as well. So you avoid the other kids who are gay. It makes it lonelier.

I didn't want to be ostracised, so I became very good at making sure that people were close to me. The idea was that when I eventually did come out, even though they would be shocked or horrified, they would still like me. I tried extra hard to make sure people were on side, that they weren't going to target me out. I wasn't friends with everyone at school, but I knew everyone's name in my year level, and that was a few hundred students.

Having to develop that skill at school has helped me a lot later on. I tend to gel with everyone, even if I'm an outsider. In that sense I get along no matter what background someone comes from. If you're highly educated, or an out-in-the-regions bogan, I can find common ground, because I've got both things in me.

I have good instincts, too. I chose good friends, in the end. All the high school friends I keep in contact with are open-minded, they've got a good sense of humour, they're tolerant. I wasn't adapting my behaviour to please them; I was adapting my behaviour because there was no other choice. You just didn't come out when I was at school. At all!

It took me a while to realise how different my experience was to most other people, that I had a unique perspective. My parents split up, I grew up Asian in a region where there were very few others, and I went through school hiding my sexuality. Later on I realised that writing was a good medium to start channelling a lot of those episodes of childhood/teenage horror.

And when I did start writing, I was very much hoping that someone like me was reading it, because I desperately wanted to read something like that when I was younger. There were so few representations on TV and in magazines of 'gay', and if you didn't want to be that big, Sydney, flashy sort of gay, there weren't any other templates.

I mean, look, I had a good set of friends, but there is another type of loneliness that comes with not being able to share the fundamental thing that defines you. I read a lot of Amy Tan, gravitated to her, because the Chinese experience wasn't really being written about in Australia.

I couldn't find any gay first-person stuff at all, so when I found David Sedaris in my late teens I f***ing devoured him. He was growing up gay and hiding it, so I could relate to him – and he was *laughing* about it. It was mind-blowing, a revelation. Now I'm conscious, when I'm writing, of trying to talk to a younger version of myself.

When you're young you are so angsty, earnest and serious. I mean, f***, I grew up in the 90s, when everyone was into grunge, and no one had a sense of irony. What I'm trying to write now is, 'Not only is that stuff hideous, but it's also funny.' You come out of it being able to laugh. It's a bit pep-talky. You know, 'It's okay to be a gaysian from a broken home.'

Leading a double life has fed into my writing. Something I learned about drama in writing school is that the most interesting thing you can get out of a character is what's going on with their private face versus their public face. The differences were really pronounced for me, and as a writer you look for those dual personalities in people. I always ask myself, 'What are you hiding?' You become a stickybeak.

I think everyone's an outsider. Everyone has a unique perspective, is utterly bizarre, has something that sets them apart. Sometimes I see a big burly footballer, a white hetero dude, who would have never felt like an outsider their entire life, speaking on TV for a pre-match interview. And I think, 'You know, you are one of the strangest creatures in the world.' ”

ADAM GOODES

They don't come much bigger, stronger or more respected than the co-captain of the Sydney Swans, Narungga man Adam Goodes, who's more decorated than Dane Swan's right arm. A dual Brownlow medallist, three times All-Australian, he skippered the Aussies in the International Rules series against Ireland, made the Indigenous Team of the Century, and was the 2010 NSW Volunteer of the Year Award Ambassador. 'Goodesy' gets coverage for all the right reasons – slamming players who engage in racial vilification, supporting the idea of gay AFL players coming out, and taking his mum to the Brownlow.

This kind of sensitivity, strength and leadership can be traced back to Adam's schooldays. His parents separated when he was four, and as the eldest of three sons he had to grow up fast. His mum, Lisa May, moved around a lot, and Adam was bounced from school to school, having to deal with a lot of new faces and a fair whack of racism.

His saviour, besides the rock solid support of Lisa May, was sport, starting out with soccer and discovering AFL in high school. Adam credits his footy mates with keeping him on track with schoolwork, protecting him from bullies, and teaching him discipline and confidence. It's not entirely clear, however, who is responsible for his voracious appetite for chocolate.

What is certain is that Adam's upbringing and school experiences made an indelible impression. He treats his status as a role model as a privilege and is determined to make a difference in disadvantaged communities. He's worked with his cousin and former team mate Michael O'Loughlin mentoring in youth detention centres, they've helped start an indigenous football academy, and co-founded the Goodes–O'Loughlin Foundation, which is dedicated to empowering the next generation of indigenous role models.

“**Growing up I went to about six** different primary schools. Going to school was very hard, because we moved quite a bit due to Mum being part of the Stolen Generation. We moved closer to family, and away from family, closer to an uncle, or aunty, that Mum was keeping in touch with, or one of Mum’s sisters that she hadn’t seen before – because she was taken away when she was five. I couldn’t even try to comprehend how hard it was for her.

Mum was looking for family ever since she realised in high school that she had other brothers and sisters that she had no idea of. She always wondered who that indigenous man was that followed her to and from school, and it was her father. You know, she really had no relationship with her mum and dad when she was taken away, and it was the biggest thing that’s affected her. Moving around was a constant thing, because she could never feel settled in the one spot.

Mum gave us so much support. She sacrificed a lot to see that we got to school, and had food in our tummies. She didn’t want us to have the upbringing she had, living in a foster family. I think, in her mind, she thought if she didn’t look after her family, the government would take her kids off her, like had happened to her mum. She didn’t want that to happen, and it’s a pretty good motivation right there. I can thank her for that, she helped me and my brothers grow into cultured young men. One of my younger brothers is a ranger in the

Grampians National Park, and my littlest brother is a player development manager, and plays reserves, with the Western Bulldogs.

I was a very shy kid. It was partly because I was born in January, so I was always one of those kids that was a lot younger than everybody else. And I wasn't sure of myself. You know, moving from place to place, meeting a new bunch of kids in class, at every school, having people look at you because you dress funny, because you look different from what they do. I just felt, 'Gee, I don't know if I want to say too much here.' It wasn't until sport that I really started to feel comfortable in my own skin and comfortable in my classes.

It wasn't until I moved to Sydney for football, and did a Diploma in Aboriginal Studies, that I realised what it actually meant to be Aboriginal.

Mostly, though, I think it was because I didn't know who I was. I actually had no idea growing up what it meant to be Aboriginal. I remember at one school we got to learn a little bit of Aboriginal language, and that was an awesome experience for me. So special. I always knew I was different from everybody else from the colour of my skin, but it wasn't until I moved to Sydney for football, and did a Diploma in Aboriginal Studies, that I realised what it actually meant to be Aboriginal.

It wasn't until high school that I first realised I was, you know … different. We moved to Horsham in country Victoria, and I think I was one of only two Aboriginal people until my brothers eventually came to high school and picked the numbers up. That's when I got the racism, the bullying from the Year 12s.

It was just stuff like … people would call me, you know, 'boong', 'coon', 'you black c***'. Whenever I walked past these particular people I could see them looking at me. They'd sometimes throw things, and would snicker things I couldn't understand, but I could tell that their attention was focused on me, and it wasn't positive energy they were focusing on me. It was very negative.

There was one kid in a year below me who just really wanted to fight me because I was Aboriginal. It didn't eventuate, but he really wanted to beat me up. I wasn't a violent kid. I wasn't an aggressive kid at all, but I was always a big kid, I had a bit of size about me, and I think that sort of protected me from getting the physical bullying, and I was very grateful for that. Most of the stuff I encountered was verbal.

When I was living in Mildura, I had to walk past this one guy's house every day to catch the bus. He would always taunt me at school, and it made me scared to walk past his place, but he'd never say anything when I actually did. I think he wanted to be cool, show me how tough he was in front of his mates.

At Horsham I had racial taunts from one guy in particular, and he would bully not just me, but he'd bully my friends into bullying me. He was very clever. While we were playing sports – footy or softball or whatever – he'd bully *them* to come and hit me, or he'd hit them. Those sorts of things.

I didn't feel completely isolated, because I had fantastic friends that accepted me, and I think the reason why was sport. It played a vital role for me and my brothers in high school. I had the natural ability to just pick up a ball, and hit it, throw it, kick it, whatever, and kids would always want me to be first or second on their team, so at a very junior level, as well, sport was the real driver for me being accepted.

Having moved from place to place, to finally settle in Horsham, it took a while, a couple of weeks into school, before I went out onto the oval. The principal had hooked me up with some people he thought I'd be like, because they were the ones hanging out at the bus shelter and smoking, those sorts of things, and that wasn't really me, so I took it upon myself to be active.

So I went outside and there were these kids kicking the footy, about 60 of them, and I went out there and took one big mark, and suddenly a group of those guys just accepted me. And as soon as footy season came around I signed up with Sunnyside, one of the local AFL sides, and that was my group of mates. All the other guys I'd become friends with were guys that I played footy against, and I think having that base of friends made it easier for me to get through the bullying. I had the benefit of having other people to talk to, other people going through my same situation, so we could talk and just laugh it off. You know, 'Oh what about that loser in Year 12 who always tries to bully us?'

I don't think I would have got through Year 12 without my friends in sport. Sport definitely gave me the confidence to do my homework and ask questions. There were a lot of kids in my situation, playing sport and trying to finish their VCE, and we'd go over to friends' houses and do our footy training, then sit around for two hours afterwards doing our homework. If I'd just gone home, I very much doubt I would have done the work. When there was a big game coming up and I was going to have to miss a day, the teachers would really support me – help me get up to speed so I wouldn't miss too much, and they'd check up on me to make sure I had my assignments done.

I had a lot of joy, you know. I had good friends who went above and beyond for me, and eventually a big family growing up that was really close. In some ways all the moving around was sort of exciting. Moving from school to school I had to adapt very quickly. It made my social skills stronger and I had to be able to come out of my shell as a child. I didn't find school easy, but I found ways of coping well, and I found it easy to learn. I thought of school as active and fun.

I remember at primary school in Adelaide, we had two teachers, and they were both PE teachers. So, if we got our work done early we'd always go outside and play games. I clearly remember that was the reward, if we finished well and on time. That system worked for me, growing up, and I still use it now. If I have a good training week, or a good patch of games, I'll do something I wouldn't usually do. You know, chocolate. Or lollies…

I hate to think how I would have turned out if I'd not been good at sport, I really do. I'm very lucky. I know sport's not it for a lot of people, but you have to find the one thing that you're good at, or want to be good at, and work towards it. Anything like that motivates you to keep going. It's important to not go through things alone, to know that lots of others go through the same difficulties, and I really recommend talking to older people about finding things that work, to help you find your place at school.

Something I had growing up, and still have, is respect for elders. I think anybody who's had more time in the world has experience and life lessons to give. If you respect these people, and ask questions, you can get through, not unscathed, but with more information under your belt.

I definitely think it's a lot harder these days. There's so much out there that's distracting, and other forms of bullying that I just can't comprehend: Facebook, the internet, Twitter, texting. I think how horrible it would have been if someone had posted pictures of me on the internet – that the whole school could see – how that would have affected me. School can still be a good experience, but children need to engage with their family, friends and teachers to really succeed. They need that support.

I didn't realise at the time, but sport taught me a lot of life lessons. For one thing, you can never perfect anything, you can always improve. That drives me. I want to get the best out of myself, for me, my family and my team, and I'm disciplined and relentless about it. I learned to not take things for granted; opportunities don't come around too often, so you need to be in the right headspace to take them. The biggest thing sport's helped me with is leadership, and understanding what sport does not just for you, but for others. When you play professional sport, you have the opportunity to really inspire people, which is actually pretty cool.

Michael and myself set up our Foundation as a vehicle to contribute back. We want to create more indigenous role models, the next young indigenous leader. We know how hard it was ourselves without support, in a disadvantaged community, to make it, so we are trying to make it a bit easier for other people. We have a target community down at the NSW/Victorian border, and we've got six fully-paid university degrees at Macquarie University here in Sydney, and we are working with Year 10, 11 and 12 kids to get them on scholarship to university. Because we all know that education is what's important – it's empowering, everything comes from there.

Growing up not knowing who I am has affected me a lot. It's a lifelong journey. I feel like I've missed out on a fantastic culture. I still believe I am part of it, but you know, not being able to speak the language, or know exactly what part of the Flinders Ranges we come from, or how big our extended family is, or where they are. I feel like I have been cheated a little bit from that point of view. But at the same time I am very proud that we are still here, adapting, and we will always be here. The best thing about our culture is that we have been able to adapt and cope. But everybody is on a journey to figure out who they are and where they come from.

Ultimately the racial abuse didn't affect me so much because I didn't understand the drive behind what people were saying. I had my cousins on the outside of school calling me 'coconut'. I didn't even know what that meant. It wasn't until I started playing AFL and being racially taunted there, that I really understood what was happening and stood up against it. That's when I said, 'That's wrong, you shouldn't say that. It actually hurts my feelings.' I went through a couple of mediation sessions with those players who vilified me to make sure they understood what they were talking about, and how it affects not just me, but my family and my extended family.

I've definitely learned to stand up for what I strongly believe in. I don't think that's negotiable. ”

JUDITH LUCY

Gold out of straw, lemonade from lemons, and Judith Lucy's enviable comedy career from the rubble of her childhood and life. It's no secret that Perth-born Judith had a challenging upbringing – as a comedian and an ex-Catholic, Jude's metier has always been the confessional – and her bestseller *The Lucy Family Alphabet* is literally an A–Z of one of the most bizarre childhoods you're going to find outside of the fantasy section of the bookshop. Or does every family keep their cat in a cage on the dinner table?

As drawn to sensitive topics as a dog to a dropped chocolate, Judith's award-winning solo comedy shows have traversed intense personal territory, such as getting fired from Austereo, hiring a gigolo and the hilarious Christmas when her sister-in-law told Judith she was adopted.

To Judith, school was a vital respite from the troubles at home, and as such she needed it that little bit too much. She'd grown up using humour to defuse tense family situations, so was able to mosey along okay at school. Most kids experience bullying as rejection from the pack, but for Jude it was the opposite; her emotional neediness saw her locked into a close friendship that did as much for her self-esteem as a fun house mirror set to 'gargoyle'.

Besides being a 22-year-plus veteran of the stand-up scene and a memoirist, Judith has starred in films (*Crackerjack* and *Bad Eggs*), done lashings of commercial radio and was a cast regular on *The D-Generation*'s iconic 90s television excursion, *The Late Show*. Her newest project, a six-part series with the ABC, is called *Judith Lucy's Spiritual Journey*, and is about her, er, spiritual journey.

“**I was a bit of a sensitive kid.** Absolutely. If someone didn’t like me I took it incredibly personally. I immediately went, ‘What’s wrong with me?’ And I think bullies pick up on that. It took a long time to work out that everyone’s got their own shit and everyone’s just trying to do their best.

From a pretty early age, when I’d hear that phrase, ‘Your schooldays are the best days of your life’, I’d think, ‘Well, I’d better blow my brains out then.’ Even though I was a fan of school, I’d just think, ‘It’s got to get better than this, doesn’t it?’ But I loved school itself because when I was there, I wasn’t at home.

Mum and Dad argued every night, so I invested a lot in school and my school friendships. But I was shy, and ill-equipped to deal with people. I never went to kindergarten because Mum was under-confident socially, and kept me at home. She didn’t think it was important for me to socialise with kids, didn’t realise it was a big deal for me when I started school. I’d only ever mixed with adults, and when I was thrown into this environment of 26 girls and four boys, I had no idea how to relate to them. I found it very difficult.

A girl who was a year older than me sussed this out pretty quickly, and in the first month or so she just scared the hell out of me. She came up to me in the playground and basically said, ‘You have to stand here, in this circle, and if you move I’ll hurt you.’ I was six, absolutely terrified, and I’d spend every recess and lunchtime standing in this circle and not moving. I finally broke down and told my mother, and she went down to the school and talked to someone and it stopped, but the fear didn't really go away.

I must admit I was struck by the 'sink or swim-ness' of school pretty quickly. I had a strong survival instinct, I think, and worked out early that you just had to get along with people. I put a lot of effort in. It made *Desperate Housewives* look like a walk in the park: god, the intrigue. Mary-Anne was my best friend for a while, and she left me for Karen, and then I became friends with Natalie, and before I knew it she'd run off with Narelle.

You just had to have a group to hang out with and I think I was also pretty desperate for a 'best' friend. Mum and Dad were wrapped up in their own world so, hey, I guess I started looking for love in all the wrong places. It wasn't until Grade 2 that I made a proper friend, Amber*, and in hindsight she was, er, a bit of a monster. We used to play these imaginary games where she was the witch, and myself and this other girl played her underlings, and she was just vile to us. She was a cow, actually, and my best friend for *years*, until the third year of high school.

After we got past primary she wasn't obviously horrible any more, she just didn't do a lot for my self-esteem. She was my antithesis. She was cool, she got breasts before everyone else, she wore make-up, went out with boys and got drunk. I was just a really uptight overachiever. A goody-good. The reality was there was so much conflict at home that I saw no point in adding to it. Why on earth would I want to inspire more shouting? I kept my head down, really, until after uni when I moved to Melbourne, and then it was 'Woohoo!'

I always wound up being a good friend to Amber's boyfriends. I was Janeane Garofalo in *The Truth About Cats & Dogs*. I was always the funny best friend who wasn't the one the boys wanted to go out with. They'd turn to me and say, 'You know, if I wasn't with Amber…' When I was 13 or 14, she said one of those lines that stays with you forever: 'You know Judith, you're *really* not attractive. But you have got a good personality.'

To the day he died my father asked after her. 'How's *Amber*?' he'd say. I'd tell him, 'I haven't seen her in years, and you know what? She didn't treat me that well', but it was always the same, 'How's that *Amber*? I *loved* that Amber.'

I used to gravitate to these intense friendships which were very toxic, where I'd constantly be seeking approval from someone who wasn't ever going to give it to me.

It was weird, because in many ways I did well. I had the lead in the school play, I was much better academically than her and yet … I don't know. She had something over me for a long time. It wasn't until late high school that I made another friend, who I genuinely got on with, and suddenly my eyes were opened. I finally realised what a true friendship could be like. I have to admit though, it does take two to tango; I mean I let myself be treated like that and she must have had her own crap going on to have behaved in that way.

You know what? In hindsight, I think with all close relationships, be it a friend or partner, they obviously bring something out in you – for good or for bad – that you want on some level. I guess I just didn't feel very good about myself, and she really confirmed that for me.

The 'Amber pattern' kept repeating for a while, to be honest. I used to gravitate to these intense friendships which were very toxic, where I'd constantly be seeking approval from someone who wasn't ever going to give it to me. They'd be dealing it out, and I'd keep coming back for more. Fortunately I wised up a few years back.

It's interesting. One of the worst decisions I made in my entire life – and I've made a few – was to go to my school reunion. It didn't help that I'd just been sacked by Austereo and my confidence was at rock bottom. I thought, 'It'll be fun, and it's been 20 years', and yet within five minutes of walking into the room I was like, 'Oh no! The reason I didn't keep in touch with any of you people is you're *all* a pack of bitches.' Okay, that's obviously an exaggeration. It was nice to see some of them but there was a lot of gossiping going on.

A lot of them were treating me oddly, kind've ignoring me, and eventually one woman walked up and said, 'Have you noticed that some of us aren't talking to you?' I said, 'Yes', and she said, 'You remember, six years ago, a bunch of us came to see your show, and we sent you a note and you didn't come out and have a drink with us?'

And you know what? I did remember that, and I explained that I hadn't come out with them because that was the night after my father disowned me, and he died six weeks later and he never spoke to me again. And she broke down and started hugging me like a crazy person, saying, 'Oh I knew there'd be a reason', and I was thinking, 'This is insane.'

I saw Amber and went up and said, 'You do realise this is what happened?' And she made me, I swear to God, juggle. Just stood there with this look on her face, and at one point casually said, 'Yeah, I heard about your parents dying, *sorry* about that.' It was like I'd gone back in time. I was trying to please her, trying to justify myself, trying to *explain*. Finally a friend grabbed me, and we left. I was sobbing, crying, and all this stuff welled up in me. Years of being treated badly, and I let myself go back there again. I couldn't believe it.

It's really, really annoying, but one thing that happens in life is that when bad shit happens to you, you *always* get something out of it. It's incredibly irritating that as you get older you realise that every cliché is true. You know how you're supposedly meant to learn from failing? Aggravatingly, it's spot on.

And, it's another cliché, but having a sense of humour is what got me through. Being able to crack jokes and make people laugh made life easier all round. Humour was a huge part of my relationship with Amber. Nothing made me feel better than making her laugh, and I used to make her laugh all the time. I was clearly chasing her approval. I created things I knew she thought were funny. There were these superhero characters, called Captain Weakling and Bog, and sometimes I'd turn up at her place dressed as Captain Weakling. I'd perform songs to try and make her laugh. I'd get a huge buzz out of doing it for her.

I'm not sure where a sense of humour comes from. Dad had a fantastic sense of humour, yet I reckon he was a bit of a bully. My mother was a lot smarter than Dad, I realised, but had no sense of humour whatsoever. But Dad just seemed to be having a lot more fun than her. He found life genuinely amusing. Maybe I did go, 'That's a great coping mechanism.'

I can see comedy as an extension of the survival instinct. For a long time I did comedy because I wanted approval. Obviously I was craving something, wanting the love from my parents that they weren't very good at showing. I eventually worked out that comedy will never fill that hole.

I look back on it all and feel very differently about it now. I loved my parents and they loved me. But it wasn't an easy childhood. Mum put me on all these crazy diets from when I was eight, so when I went to other people's houses I'd eat like a maniac. We'd watch some television, and then, as opposed to everyone else in my year, I wasn't allowed to stay the night. She was weirdly overprotective. Two hours after dinner and Mum would be at the door.

There was no point trying to hide my home situation. I went to the same school for 12 years – people already knew how 'interesting' my parents were. But I saw uni as a new beginning, and when someone would drop me home, I'd always say, 'Oh, anywhere around here', blocks from where I lived.

I remember a friend being left alone in the kitchen, reaching into the cupboard to pull out a coffee cup and literally screaming. Because Mum had put a cup back on the shelf several weeks ago with coffee still in it, and it was this fetid… That would happen all the time. Mum wasn't big on housekeeping. I just wanted to get people out of the house as soon as possible.

I think, also, in terms of my career, because I came from an extraordinarily secretive family, my reaction has been to go tell everything. There were so many things that were never spoken about, like me being adopted. Maybe a part of my brain's missing, but when I hear that someone's a very private person, I always think, 'Why? What's the point? We're all in this shit together. We all f*** up. We all make mistakes. We've all got skeletons in the closet. Let's talk about it.'

This industry has been very kind to me. And if I hadn't had the difficulties, and the massive insecurity and desperate need for approbation, I maybe wouldn't have gone into it, and I wouldn't have been so driven. I've worked some stuff out now, there's a level of desperation I used to have that I don't have any more, and I can enjoy the good stuff about being a comedian. Maybe the way I got here wasn't so great, but where I am now is really good. I genuinely do love making people laugh.

My brother, Niall, is older than me and when I came to the end of school I told him how sad I was, convinced I'd miss everyone. And he said, 'No you won't. You'll never see most of those people again. Your friends will be the ones you meet at uni, because you'll share the same interests.' And I was going, 'No! No! Nooo! I'll be friends with all these people forever!'

And, of course, he was entirely correct. ”

**not her real name.*

PAUL CAPSIS

It's been said that the reviews of Australia's premier cabaret artiste Paul Capsis read like religious awakenings. Somewhat ironic since he gave Catholicism the flick 30 years ago, but such is his onstage power and wounded charisma that admirers reach for 'transcendent', 'transformative' and 'voice of an angel', before slowing to a halt and gazing off transfixed into the middle distance.

As far from the traditional Aussie archetype as lobster mornay is from little lunch, Paul has made his mark on stages worldwide, from Vienna to Hong Kong, in plays and operas, and opposite Alex Dimitriades in the film *Head On*. But he's most acclaimed for his striking, award-winning solo cabaret shows, where he showcases his supremely versatile singing voice and ability to channel damaged divas from Billie Holiday to Janis Joplin.

As a slight, sunny, softly spoken Maltese–Greek Australian boy growing up in Sydney with his grandmother in the 1970s, Paul experienced bullying so severe that it hindered his learning. If being gay is problematic *now*, back then it was an invitation for mistreatment so savage it made an episode of *Oz* look like afternoon tea with Justin Bieber. Oh, and wogs weren't exactly flavour of the month, either.

Paul credits music with saving him through school, but with the benefit of hindsight, credits school for shaping him into the potent, determined, unique talent he is today.

“**There was no bullying in the first** three years. I went to a Catholic school and I was in love with the nuns. I thought the world was wonderful, people were nice, and everyone was free to sing and dance like the Elvis movies I watched on TV. But then Mum couldn’t afford to send me there any more, and when I was eight I went to a public school in the same suburb, Surry Hills, and it was *rough*, with a huge mix of cultures – Lebanese, Turkish, Aboriginal, everything.

From when I arrived there were comments: ‘You sound like my sister’, ‘You sound like my mother’, ‘You’re a girl, you’re not really a boy.’ But it was a magical time. I had a wonderful teacher who’d play Beatles records and wanted us to dance and sing and perform. Because of my Greek heritage, when we’d go to parties there’d be Turkish music and belly dancing, and this teacher, my favourite, encouraged me to belly dance in front of the school at assembly.

That was … a huge mistake. She put on a track with sitar music from the *Sgt. Pepper’s* album, and I got up, on my own, in my school uniform – in my *greys* – and did this dancing. It was hideous. *Terrible*. Everything changed; I was picked on every day. It was so full on.

And it went on, and on, and on. From teachers, too. I had a racist teacher in Year 6 who picked on my brother and me because we were ‘non-Australian’. So there was the wog thing, and the girly thing. I was eight when I first heard the word ‘poofter’. I didn’t know what it was, but I knew it was bad, because people *hated* me for it. A Greek boy said to me once, 'If I was like you, I would want my father to kill me. You're a disgrace to the Greeks.'

There were these brothers who used to wait for me after school finished, to hit and kick me. Sometimes just one little hit, one little kick and then walk away. They bashed my brother Manuel too, once. Not because he was a poofter. Because he had *asthma*. They saw us coming, basically. My father didn't raise us, so we didn't have that male thing, what to do in a fight. I had no idea. We weren't brought up with any guidance about how to protect yourself in a physical way.

Manuel's 18 months older than me, and they made his nose bleed. I became hysterical, and screamed and shouted, and they freaked and stopped hitting him. This lying in wait thing went on for a while, but one day I'd had enough and defended myself. I went crazy, I laid into this boy, and a woman ran across the road and told me off. She called me a bully, and shouted at me to leave him alone. I'd begun developing this behaviour where I'd take it, take it, take it, and then I'd explode. They were clever enough not to hit or kick me where they could be caught, but when I retaliated, full of fury, it would be in front of the teacher and I'd get punished.

There was a Portuguese boy who would, every day, just slap me in the face. One day I picked him up, grabbed him by the collar and threw him so hard he went flying into chairs and tables, and then I burst into tears. We both got the cane.

I'd go into my mum's room and look in her dressing-table mirror, and stare at myself, for ages. I thought, 'There's something there that everyone sees but I don't. And if I look in the mirror I'll find it.' If I could find it, I thought, I could *change* it.

My grandmother raised me and Manuel. Mum lived nearby, more an older sister-type figure; someone I'd see every day, but she was there and gone. Discipline and leave. She was a black sheep, because of having two children and no husband. In her family, that was *big*. Dad was supposed to pay, but for whatever reason we wore hand-me-downs, Smith Family clothes. Our clothes were mismatched and odd, and I wore jackets from different schools.

So, pretty much, I was threatened a lot. And then, because I was still 11 at the end of the Sixth Grade, they made me repeat a year. There were about nine of us who were the wrong age for high school. With the news that I had to stay there, with that horrible teacher, at that dreadful school, I told my grandmother I wasn't going back.

I'd heard about this other school, about five blocks away, and I went there by myself to meet the teachers, to find out if I could go there. I was in the Surry Hills area, so they said yes. My mother said, 'No! You're not going there. You're not walking that far to school.' But my grandmother said to let me.

I had the best six months of my school life there. It was the polar opposite of the other place. The teachers were friendly and nice. The kids were nice. Everyone sang, everyone performed, everyone got on. I couldn't believe this place existed. I remember thinking, 'Why didn't I come here before?' I was absolutely devastated on my last day. I hid under the stairs and sobbed.

My brother was already at the high school I was going to, and he'd told me, 'All those boys are waiting for you. They told me, they're going to get you.' And I went to this school and it was everything my brother said. But worse.

It was a jail, built by convicts, and part of it still was a jail. The whole vibe of the school was jail. The teachers were like wardens, and the boys were out of control. The first thing I remember seeing was the woodwork teacher being chased by a class of boys across the grounds. I thought, 'If they can do that to a teacher, I'm f***ed.' And I was. It was ridiculous.

Nothing happened for six months, so I thought it was just a threat, but then it started, and it was every day. It was a nightmare. Even the teachers, especially the sports teachers. I'd go along to sports and do everything, but each time I was violently abused, and it just escalated. By Year 9 it was absolutely out of control. Even the headmaster was mortified by me.

In all the six years I spent there, I could not go into the playground. If I did I'd get water thrown on me, or kicked. I was called 'poofter' or 'faggot' every day. I was spat on. Clothes ripped. Punched. Hair pulled. By Year 9 I could only go to the toilet during class, when no one was around. But there was the odd kid who *would* be around. And they'd get me. This Turkish boy just came up once and punched me in the face. Said nothing. Just punched me and walked off.

I couldn't learn because I was anxious the whole time. I just couldn't learn. Every day was about how to get through the day. How do I survive until I get home? It was terrifying. My fantasy was, 'How can I become invisible?' Because there were boys who *were* kind've invisible. They didn't pull any attention at all. I dreamed of that. I tried once, cutting my hair really short like the others, and dressing like them, but I still had my voice and I was still *me*. It didn't work. It was still the same. So I went, 'Oh well, f*** it.'

I didn't have strategies, apart from *not* being out in the playground. I knew I couldn't be outside. But there were teachers that were very good to me, and it helped. Over the years, as the violence got worse, some of them – my art, music and English teachers – went to great lengths to help and protect me. They'd lock me in the art room during recess. But of course, sometimes you'd go to class and the teacher wasn't there yet. It might only be five minutes, but that's all they needed to get me.

The worst day of my life was in Year 9. I was in art class and the teacher was late – it was funny, because she was one who protected me – but a boy hit me, or said something, and I picked up this broom handle and whacked him with it. That's when the teacher walked in, and I got in trouble. She threw me out of the class. I lost it. I smashed the window. I wanted to jump. We were on the third floor. I would've died, and I wanted to. Being hated by so many people at once, all the time; it does your head in. I got cut. There was blood and glass everywhere. I was a mess, an absolute mess. The teacher was so, so sorry. I was standing there sobbing, covered in blood. They left me alone for a little while after that. They went, 'He's nuts.'

Year 9 was intense. Pretty severe. I got bashed by another group of older, football-playing boys. I was doing my usual avoiding thing, going through the corridors when no one else was around, and I ran into these boys who'd just come out of class. They bashed and kicked me in the corridor. I had my first out-of-body experience. My body left me and I observed what was happening – and I felt *nothing*. I was completely numb.

I threw my schoolbag, I ran out of the school. I didn't look; I was just running. It was on a busy street, this school; I could have been killed. My mother went and saw the principal, and because I knew some of those boys' names, they got badly punished. They got like nine whips of the cane, and didn't touch me again.

I wanted to leave, but my English teacher told my mother not to let me. He said, 'You'll have this problem wherever he goes. It will disrupt his education, and the other boys are starting to mature.' So I stayed. I was the first one in my family to ever do Year 12. Not one single member of my family had done their HSC before. My brother had left. He hated it, he couldn't cope, and after Year 9 he was gone.

I was determined, because I didn't want to be a cleaner. I didn't want to do those physical, menial jobs like my family. After Year 10 my grandmother said to me, 'Y'know you've probably had enough school now. Get out of there now.' And I said, 'No, it's better now', and I stayed. Which I found bizarre even to myself.

Things *had* changed by Year 10. It was a bit better. A lot of the violent boys left after Year 9; my real problems, the real bad cases, they went out into the workforce. There was a different energy; I was older, and by then I had developed a very tough sort of persona. I got a reputation; if you hassled me, you'd get the tongue. You'd get a piece.

I'd developed the comeback, and I'd stand my ground and give it to them. Unsparingly. I wanted them to feel what I felt. I'd attack them: their physicality, their family – I'd go all out. I publicly took on the gay thing, and had some fun with it. If someone hassled me I'd say, 'Yeah, I *am* gay, but I wouldn't suck *your* cock. That tiny thing!' They'd be, 'You're mad!' I was incredibly defiant, even though I hadn't had sex, I hadn't done anything with anyone.

I really rebelled, and music was a *massive*, massive factor. It saved me. I would go home after school, turn off the lights, and lie in my bedroom and listen to Janis Joplin. There was something in her voice that helped me, that gave me strength. The way she sang, the way she *screamed*, something in her voice was like an angel with big wings. She helped me from the grave.

Janis was my hero, my role model. I read about her, and she was bullied. At university they voted her 'ugliest man on campus', and we're talking Texas in the late 50s. And the more stuff they did, the more defiant and the tougher she became. She was *so* defiant. As my obsession with her escalated, that's when I became very 'Janis' tough. Yeah. I'm gonna wear a vest, and my hair long, f*** you.

She was my armour. In all the quotes I read she said, 'I'm gonna be myself, I don't give a shit. I'm *me*. I don't care!' That's what I grabbed onto. I thought, 'Well, they're telling me I'm different too. They all hate me too. But look at her, she's a *rock star*.' She was powerful. And that's kind of what inspired me to perform, as well. I was into any women singers who were tough. That's what I liked. Because my grandmother was very strong and tough, and my mother too. They're 'no shit' women.

I remember praying a lot when I was a child. Praying for people to stop hitting me. Praying really hard. So by 17, I was like, this religion thing is *bullshit*. I'm gay, and I wanna have nothing to do with this hateful thing that tries to make me scared, with its heaven and hell and good and bad. *Hateful*.

I think I made it because I developed some fight, and because there was support. There were a few kind people around, and sometimes that's all you need.

Coming to terms with being gay was very difficult. When I was 17, and realised I *was* gay, I didn't accept it. I had a lot of self-hatred going on. I was very depressed, suicidal, because I thought life was bleak. I was gay and hated. I'd try saying to myself, 'No, no. You're not. Really, you're not.' But I was. And I didn't want to be gay. I hated it. Other kids have fun in high school, sexually experimenting. Not me. Being 'gay' brought so much misery, the last thing I wanted to do was engage in it. I was terrified and confused. Part of me thinks, 'Oh, I wish I'd had some fun', but it wasn't safe for me.

A couple of times I was violently approached at school by older boys, one of them pushing me to the floor of a toilet cubicle and screaming, 'Suck my cock!' He had his pants down and was frothing at the mouth. There was a bit of that. But there were also these wonderful teachers who would talk to me, and say, 'It's okay if you are gay.'

I was very late in learning because of all the anxiety, but in Years 10, 11 and 12, because I could finally relax, my brain started taking in information, and I was coming first in things like art, ancient history and geography. And I had teachers I looked up to, who I loved, and who loved me. I think I made it because I developed some fight, and because there was support. There were a few kind people around, and sometimes that's all you need.

I'm glad I stayed on till Year 12. Because it did shift, it did change. And that's why I'm talking about this now, because I've been hearing a lot about bullying and suicides. But even without suicide, it's about how bullying scars you. And you've got to deal with that shit. You can't have that experience and then expect for it not to impact. I look back now and realise, of *course* enduring abuse like that has some kind of long-term effect.

When I left high school I was very, very, *very* f***ing angry. For *years* I was so angry. Then, through my twenties, I went through a forgiveness. I thought about it a lot, tried to figure out *why* they were so cruel, and I felt sad for those boys. Like, what were *they* going through to do that to someone else? They were having shit in their own lives; I think their parents were violent.

I had therapy, because I thought I'd dealt with it, but I hadn't. I had no self-confidence, no self-esteem. I was hated for so long, why would anyone want me? And I'd just come out and started having relationships, and then it was the AIDS crisis. I thought, 'Wow. I'm being *punished*.' I was too scared to do anything with anyone. In my late twenties I started having panic attacks, and they were pretty severe. A couple of times I took myself to hospital, because I thought I was dying. So I had to do something. I started meditation, I read self-help books, and I began therapy.

But my life started after I finished high school. It's like I was born then. Everything changed. In the years after school, gradually people became my friends, and they thought I was funny, and they liked me. And I had one friend from primary school, Mark, a tall Anglo guy, and he stayed my friend right through high school even though it meant he copped it too. He's the one who got me into community theatre when I left school. I joined Shopfront Theatre, and the five years I spent there was the first experience, other than the six months at that school I found for myself, where I thought maybe the world was okay.

I'm very grateful to the theatre, because it educated me. It made up for years of not being able to learn, because I was in a world where I had to absorb information, and research, and learn scripts. I also credit my grandmother's upbringing, because she was a fiercely determined woman. She had no education. She told me, 'You have to go to school or you'll be like me, not able to read or write.' But she worked three jobs and she had six kids. I felt safe with her, and she raised me to *work*.

To be really honest, because I made it that way, school became a positive learning experience for me. It made me wary and distrustful of people, but it toughened me, gave me a more realistic view of what humanity is about. I have a very, very low tolerance for bad behaviour or disloyalty. If people cross me, betray me, backstab me, dishonour me or whatever, it's *over*. Anything dodgy in relationships, I leave. We're not here for long, and I want to surround myself with beautiful people. And you can make that choice.

There was a lesson in it. It gave me a real sense of survival, of not giving up; I wasn't going to allow people to stop me. That's come in useful. Everybody said to me that I'd never make it as a performer. Because I'm a wog. Because I'm a poofter. Because I'm girly. The list went on. You're short. You're big nosed. Everything. I got it all. But I persisted. Because I'm incredibly stubborn and determined. I thought, 'Y'know what? If it's true I don't accept it. I'm gonna do it anyway.'

It's shaped me. Everything I've done as a performer has gone a long way from what I was supposed to be. I started creating my own cabaret work in my twenties, and that's what I'm now known for. Because I was like, 'Yeah, I'm just gonna be me. I've got to create my own work.' Every artist I admire didn't follow a pattern; they were groundbreakers. And now I see people copying me, doing bits of my stuff; I see that coming up now, which is fabulous. And I've had lots of young people over the years write to me – girls, boys, gay, straight, wog, Anglo. They relate.

I don't need people's blessing like I used to. I don't have that incredible need to be liked. I accept that I will be unliked, and liked. That's the world. And I like my life now. I've had some difficult things to deal with, but it's never stopped me from being who I am.

I distinctly remember thinking, after wanting to kill myself, that I was going to do the opposite. *Because* I'm so hated, I'm going to do everything in my power to have a good life and not self-destruct. I'm not going to do to myself what's been done to me. That's why I haven't done drugs. I was clear minded about wanting to be an artist, and I wasn't going to let addiction get in the way. I'm surprised at how determined and adamant about choices I've been.

I'm so glad now that I didn't self-harm, that I didn't kill myself. Oh my god. I would have missed out on a lot of fabulous life. A lot of incredible experiences. I'm very grateful I've had them, as an artist and as a person.

I'm becoming more powerful as I get older, and I hardly think about those times now. I'm not the same person I was five years ago, ten years ago. For sure. I'd have loved to have been like I am now in my twenties, or in school. It would have been very different. But what's the point of saying that? Because all that had to happen for me to get to here. ”

BRENDAN COWELL

Brendan Cowell is remarkable. Sure, he's an award-winning actor and scriptwriter, and recently had his first novel published, but what's most impressive is that at school he managed to be good at sport and *still* deeply unpopular. That takes talent.

Born and bred in Cronulla, NSW, and living with three women from the age of 13, Brendan was a poor fit at his all-boys school from the start, foisting personal poetry and dance routines on his highly resistant schoolmates. He was regarded as suspiciously as an abandoned suitcase at the airport.

This state of affairs escalated when he started appearing on telly. A high profile is a mixed blessing at any school. Intriguingly, despite being routinely ostracised and taunted, Brendan didn't change his behaviour one iota and kept right on reading his poetry out at assembly and putting on peculiar shows.

In the end Brendan's strategy paid off. By the time he graduated he'd gone from being the freak to one of the cool guys, and kids came to see his plays instead of calling him names from a distance. This insistence on staying true to himself has translated into a rich, prolific and satisfying career.

Brendan has written nine plays, including *Ruben Guthrie* and *Bed*, which won the Patrick White Playwright's Award. He starred in the TV series *Love My Way,* and the films *Noise*, *Beneath Hill 60* and *I Love You Too*. His novel, *How It Feels*, is a dark coming-of-age based on his experiences and observations growing up in Cronulla.

“**I was a weirdo.** Everyone just thought I was a bit of a weirdo. At primary school I was into cricket and rugby league, basketball and stuff, but when I'd invite boys from school over, I'd want to choreograph a dance routine to 'The Power Of Love' by Huey Lewis and the News, and they'd just want to go fishing or terrorise something. I was always wanting to make little plays, and entertain and stuff, and they'd be like, 'Why do you want to do a f***ing dance routine for?' I think I freaked everybody out.

A couple of the guys stopped asking me over as much, and I was skateboarding with a gang, and all of a sudden I didn't know where they were skateboarding. A few guys didn't want to come over anymore because I wanted to dance with them. They probably thought it was a bit gay or something.

But ever since I can remember, on Friday nights, I got my nan and my mum and we'd have Red Faces like that thing on *Hey Hey It's Saturday*. I was four or five, and I was all the contestants on Red Faces – I'd have five things prepared – and they had to pick a winner. I'd have, like, a Michael Jackson impersonation, then a poem I'd written called something like 'Staring at Puddles'. Then I'd sing 'Shaddup Your Face', and, um, tell them a story, and impersonate someone from my school. I mean, seriously, what was I doing? But I've always been, 'Hey, you gotta watch this!' I just wanted to get in front of people.

I got into telly by accident. I spent a lot of time in my youth, with my mum, waiting outside dance studios and ballet halls for my sisters. We were in this waiting room one time, and there were like 20 kids who looked like me, blue eyes and chubby cheeks, and one by one they were going off into this room. And then a guy came out and said, 'Right, okay, you're next', and I was like, 'What?' But I went in, and ate some cornflakes, and said, 'Yum', and the guy went, 'You've got a good head, kid, who's your agent?' And I said, 'What's an agent?' So he hooked me up with an agent, I got the cornflakes ad, and I was away. Eating and smiling on television.

So I was in and out with friends at primary school, but it wasn't too bad. But as soon as I turned ten, till I was about 15, it was really hard. From when I was on the telly a bit, that's when the bad times started. It was a very lonely few years; I had no friends and it was pretty depressing. The guys at school figured that if you're on telly you think you're better than everyone. I didn't think that. I was just making money, having fun, and it made me feel good. I definitely didn't flaunt it.

But then I'd go to school and everyone'd make a big deal of it, make fun of me, and terrorise me. I had some scary walks home, with kids I knew forming circles around me, yelling and calling me names.

I was doing TV ads, for Pavlova Magic, and Crisco Oil, and My Juice is Fruity, and kids would form a circle around me, and sing the ad, and push me around. Other kids would call me 'moo cow'. About 30 of them would get around me and moo at me, like cows, all the way to getting my bike. It sounds silly, but at the time it's really scary.

I remember turning down a couple of things, because I just kept thinking, 'If I do that, what will they sing? What will happen?' Particularly when I got the Combantrin commercial. I would have had to say, 'I've got worms', and I thought, 'I can't do that.' Can you imagine? 'I've got worms', and then going to school the next day? I would have been crucified. So I turned it down for my own protection, even though it was like $5000.

It gets to you. I mean, it's the weekend, and everyone else is over at their mate's house, and been invited to parties, and you're just hanging with your mother. On a Saturday!

For a long time I was really sad, really alone. Just riding my bike home on my own, and walking back through the bush on my own, and day after day seeing everyone hanging out having icy poles, riding their boards, and me thinking, '*Nobody* wants to hang out with me. Like no one. Everybody hates me.'

I really couldn't make a friend; I kept trying. I had one friend in kindergarten who was Vietnamese, and he was my best friend for four years, but his family were boat people so they got deported back to Vietnam when he was in Year 6. And he was it until Year 9. It gets to you. I mean, it's the weekend, and everyone else is over at their mate's house, and been invited to parties, and you're just hanging with your mother. On a Saturday!

I had some really dark thoughts. I thought all sorts of things. I thought I was a freak, and I thought about running away, and I thought about dying. I thought I was a pain to everyone. It was awful. I know my mother was incredibly worried about me. She was getting me to read books, get into theatre, and trying to fill my head with ideas of another land, another place, a life out of the Shire and out of the school.

I was starting to be on TV more and more. I was hosting an afternoon show with Cameron Daddo, and doing breakfast TV and I was on *A Country Practice* or *Sons and Daughters* and you know, I was on telly a fair bit.

I started to have a bit of a voice at school and it wasn't exactly welcomed. I was writing poetry and reading it at assembly, and doing weird performance stuff, which is not gonna help your cause. Not in Cronulla. I created a suggestion box in the library and at assembly. I said, um, 'I want to know all the suggestions of things that students want at the school; we can put money in for charities, we can have entertainment nights or talent quests.' I said that I'd pool the suggestions, and approach the staff and see if we could get some fundraising for things that the students want in the school.

And everyone just wrote, 'I suggest Brendan Cowell should just get f***ed', 'I suggest we should have a surfing competition and Brendan Cowell should get f***ed', and, ah, 'I think Brendan Cowell is gay, and I suggest you go and suck a dick.' They weren't exactly, you know, what I was hoping for.

One day this guy, who was the captain of the rugby union team, got this rumour going that he was going to fight me on the oval at 3.30pm. I didn't even know him, and the whole school was going, 'You're going to fight this guy', and I thought he was going to kill me. Now, this is a pretty wimpy thing to do, but I went to the principal's office, and I said, 'Hey, um, this guy wants to fight me today, and I don't really know him and I don't want to fight him.' And the principal of the school looked at me and said, 'Well, there's certain things a man has to do to be respected by his peers', and he just walked off. I mean, what?!

So I rolled up. I went, 'Hey man, I don't want to fight you', and he came up and smacked me in the head twice. I fell over and said, 'You win, man', shook his hand, got on my bike and rode off. Weirdly, a lot of people respected me after that.

After my parents divorced at 13 I spent most of my time with Mum and my two sisters, and my nan, and they were all strong, opinionated, kinda alpha women, so I didn't have problems talking with women. Our school took girls in from Year 10, and the guys started looking at me going, 'Holy shit, Brendan Cowell is talking to the girls.' I was just talking to them; I didn't have a lot of action, but I had a lot of female company.

I was pretty charming with the ladies early on, you know? I was vice captain of my school (due to the fact only a couple of us put our names in for election), and I'd do debating, we'd have meetings with other schools, and all the girls who were valedictorians and school captains really liked me. 'Cause I was cheeky and smart and I wasn't like all the other dopey guys at school who just sneered at girls or worse.

It all changed when I met Johnny, this Scottish guy, who had pimples all over his face, and had just arrived in the country. We instantly became friends. And then there was Bart, a big six-foot-four guy who kinda looked after me a lot. Then suddenly our good looks started forming, Johnny's pimples went away, we formed a band and it just made everything cool and better.

We started going to rave parties and wearing baggy pants and stripey shirts, and all of a sudden everyone wanted to know what we were doing. They heard we were going to nightclubs and hanging out with girls, and taking our parents' cars out, and all of a sudden everyone was like, 'Holy shit, these are the coolest guys in the school.' And we were! All of a sudden we were very popular. We had an air of mystique about us, we became a bit dangerous and a bit cool and a bit revered.

By Year 11 I was dating the hottest girl in Year 11, I was putting plays on and people were coming to see them, and I'd get up and speak at assembly and they'd applaud me, you know. So I went from being the kid that got laughed at, and mocked, and ostracised and all that shit to, 'That's that Cowellf***ing guy.' It turned right around for me.

I think it was because I never stopped being who I was, you know? I didn't go, 'Okay, I'll be like the rest of you.' I thought, 'F*** ya, I'm going to be me, and I'm going to take it, and take it, and take it, until you accept it.' Then they accepted it and they wanted to be a part of it.

And I kept being myself because I didn't know what else to do. My mum told me not to stop being myself, and I had this burning thing in me. I thought, 'Well, you've made me the weirdo, you've made me the outcast, and so I will be.'

I took a lot from that period. It's made me who I am. I think you gotta hang onto your voice, and you'll be rewarded. If your voice is pure it'll find its place eventually, as much as people try to drown it out, trample on it, and make it sound more like theirs and more like everybody else's.

Australians in general like affable people and harmless people and it was the same at school. Don't shine, don't be special, don't be irregular, and don't do anything that's not in line with everybody else. I didn't listen to that, so I got punished, and even now, I feel as an artist I say too much about the problems in this country.

I just wrote a novel about youth suicide in Cronulla, because it's got the highest youth suicide rate in the country, and a lot of my friends took their own lives when I was at school. People from where I'm from really don't like that

I've done it. But *someone*'s got to say it, and – maybe it's from that time – I just went, 'F*** it, I'm going to be that guy.' I might be ostracised or unpopular, but it's a choice you make to put yourself in that part of society, and I think I made it early on.

It's hard to have perspective when you're young – you can't shoot out of your life and look at it. I reckon that's why a lot of kids take their lives. If a girl dumps you at school and everyone laughs at you, you don't know that you'll have 20 more girlfriends, then marry a beautiful woman that you'll meet on holiday in Bali in eight years time, have three children, and be successful in what you do.

You just think, 'This is the end of the f***ing world', and that every feeling you're having right now are the only feelings you'll ever have, you'll never escape them, and that's the end. I had those thoughts but I somehow got through. But I had a mother and a father who kept telling me I had something to give, and one of those drama teachers who went, 'You've got to make waves, you've got something.' Even if they're the minority, a couple of those people can really change your life.

I'm grateful to all those guys that dumped me in the urinal, threw eggs at my head, 'mooed' me, called me names and chased me out of the school grounds. All of it. Yeah. I see them now, when I go to Cronulla, and they're fat and bending corrugated iron in the factory. And I don't think, 'F*** you, look who won.' I just think, 'You never grew.'

They never challenged themselves, never got out, never went through anything. They just picked on everyone that was different, and I was different, and they didn't stop me. And that's the important thing: find a way to not let people stop you being who you are. ”

ACKNOWLEDGEMENTS

Firstly, I'd like to thank everyone who agreed to be interviewed for *Don't Peak At High School.* One of the flipsides to being a 'successful Australian' is that spare time is scarcer than panda triplets, and, as demonstrated by the empirically proven 'fame' algorithm, the less time you have available, the more people clamour for a piece of you.

So I truly appreciate that these brave, talented, high-achieving folk prioritised contributing to the book. Bullying is a scourge – always has been, always will be – and everyone was passionate about sharing their experiences in the hope it offered solace, inspiration or perspective. And what stories! I've felt utterly privileged conducting these interviews, and have been blown away by people's honesty, openness and generosity. I never thought I'd be thanking people for making me cry, but there's hardly a story in this book which didn't break my heart one way or another.

I also couldn't, quite literally, have completed this book without a lot of help from my friends. Due to, depending on how you frame it, chronic time mismanagement or an unavoidable clash of major creative deadlines (I favour the latter interpretation, but then, I would), it was a temporal impossibility for me transcribe most of the interviews.

Several friends stepped up to the metaphoric plate, and given that transcribing is almost unutterably arduous, I cannot thank them enough. Particularly Karen Teague and Cathy Reid, given that they'd never done it before, and yet demonstrated grace and intestinal fortitude in the face of the discovery that, yes, one interview can take 15 hours to transcribe. In no particular order of valour – they're all champions to me – unlimited gratitude also goes out to Melissa Cranenburgh, Sabian Wilde, Halley Metcalfe, Andrew McIlraith, Monique Brasher, Meredith King, Lou Pardi and Tracy Routledge. Legends one and all.

And thanks to my long-suffering publisher, Martin Hughes. For founding Affirm Press, a publishing company which aims to do good in the world, for leaping enthusiastically all over this project, and for not hassling me much despite deadlines whipping past like telegraph poles out of a train window.

And to my lovely boyfriend Greg, for the hugs and dinners.

RESOURCES

Kids Helpline

Free confidential telephone, email and online counselling service for 5 to 25 year olds

kidshelp.com.au

1800 55 1800

Lifeline Australia

Free 24-hour telephone and web counselling service

lifeline.org.au

13 11 44

Headroom

Information on mental health by young people, for young people

headroom.net.au

Bullying. No Way!

School communities working together against bullying

bullyingnoway.com.au

Youthbeyondblue

A not-for-profit organisation working to address depression, anxiety and related disorders for 12 to 25 year olds

youthbeyondblue.com

Friendly Schools

An evidence-based bullying prevention program

friendlyschools.com.au

Headspace

The national youth mental health foundation

headspace.org.au

The Alannah and Madeline Foundation

A national charity keeping children safe from violence

amf.org.au

National Centre Against Bullying

Information about creating safe schools and communities

ncab.org.au

Mind Matters

A government-funded mental health initiative for secondary school students

mindmatters.edu.au

Reach Out Australia

A web-based service providing mental health information and support to young people

au.reachout.com

Peer Support Foundation

Peer-led programs that foster mental, physical and social wellbeing

peersupport.edu.au